PALO MAYOMBE
THE GARDEN OF
BLOOD & BONES

NICHOLAJ DE MATTOS FRISVOLD · BIBLIOTHÈQUE ROUGE · MMXI

PALO MAYOMBE
THE GARDEN OF
BLOOD & BONES

A GRAMMARY OF THE CREOLE SORCERY OF PALO MAYOMBE

Published by Scarlet Imprint
under the *Bibliothèque Rouge* banner
/rouge

Copyright © Nicholaj de Mattos Frisvold, 2010
Edited by Peter Grey
Design © *At-Tāriq*
ISBN 978-0-9567203-9-9
Printed & bound in Great Britain by
CPI Antony Rowe

CONTENTS

ACKNOWLEDGMENTS

Some people have proved instrumental in their constant encouragement and I feel it is proper to give a special thanks to Mambo Mama Tida Choukêt, Anaia Xabier, Jake Stratton-Kent and, of course, Peter and Alkistis.

May you all live well and prosper now and forever more!

INTRODUCTION

Palo Mayombe is perhaps best known for its display of human skulls in iron cauldrons and accompanied by necromantic practices that contribute to its eerie reputation of being a cult of antinomian and hateful sorcerers. This murky reputation is from time to time reinforced by uninformed journalists and moviemakers who present Palo Mayombe in similar ways as Vodou has been presented through the glamour and horror of Hollywood. It is the age old fear of the unknown and of powers that threaten the established order that are spawned from the umbra of Palo Mayombe. The cult is marked by ambivalence replicating an intense spectre of tension between all possible contrasts, both spiritual and social. This is evident both in the history of Kongo inspired sorcery and practices as well as the tension between present day practitioners and the spiritual conclaves of the cult. Palo Mayombe can be seen either as a religion in its own right or a Kongo inspired cult. This distinction perhaps depends on the nature of ones *munanso* (temple) and *rama* (lineage). Personally, I see Palo Mayombe as a religious cult of Creole Sorcery developed in Cuba. The Kongolese heritage derives from several different and distinct regions in West Africa that over time saw a metamorphosis of land, cultures and religions giving Palo Mayombe a unique expression in its variety, but without losing its distinct nucleus. In the history of Palo Mayombe we find elite families of Kongolese aristocracy that contributed to shaping African history and myth, conflicts between the Kongolese and explorers, with the Trans-Atlantic slave trade being the blood red thread in its development.

The name Palo Mayombe is a reference to the forest and nature of the Mayombe district in the upper parts of the deltas of the Kongo River, what used to be the Kingdom of Loango. For the European merchants, whether sent by the Church to convert the people or by a king greedy for land and natural resources, everything south of present day Nigeria to the beginning of the Kalahari was simply Kongo. This un-nuanced perception was caused by the linguistic similarities and of course the prejudice towards these 'savages' and their 'primitive' cultures.

To write a book about Palo Mayombe is a delicate endeavor as such a presentation must be sensitive both to the social as well as the emotional memory inherited by the religion. I also consider it important to be true to the fundamental metaphysical principles of the faith if a truthful presentation of the nature of Palo Mayombe is to be given. The few attempts at presenting Palo Mayombe outside ethnographic and anthropological dissertations have not been very successful. They have been rather fragmented attempts demonstrating a lack of sensitivity not only towards the cult itself, but also its roots. Consequently a poor understanding of Palo Mayombe has been offered, often borrowing ideas and concepts from Santeria and Lucumi to explain what is a quite different spirituality. I am of the opinion that Palo Mayombe should not be explained on the basis of the theological principles of Santeria. Santeria is Yoruba inspired and not Kongo inspired and thus one will often risk imposing concepts on Palo Mayombe that distort a truthful understanding of the cult. To get down to the marrow; Santeria is a Christianized form of a Yoruba inspired faith – something that should make the great differences between Santeria and Palo Mayombe plain. Instead, Santeria is read into Palo Mayombe and the cult ends up being presented at best in a distorted form. I will accordingly refrain from this form of syncretism and rather present Palo Mayombe as a Kongo inspired cult of Creole Sorcery that is quite capable of standing on its own three legs without borrowing ideas and concepts from its Yoruba inspired cousin, Santeria. The reference to Palo Mayombe as Creole Sorcery is a term that reflects both the contemporary consensus as well as the tension between the Yoruba and the Kongo worldview. The Yoruba people always took pride in their sophisticated religious ways while looking down on their neighbors to the south, north and east, often seeing them as vulgar in their spiritual ways. Continuing in this vein, we find even today Yoruba people defining the practices found in Kongo and Benin as 'charming ways' with clearly negative implications.

My own encounter with Palo Mayombe started in the early 90s when I obtained contact with some practitioners of Palo Mayombe from Puerto Rico and Miami. These encounters turned out to be quite disappointing at first, but in time rewarding in their own right. I was intrigued with the whole idea of the nganga, the spirit pot, seeing this as the genuine witch's cauldron. My vision of the nganga was accompanied by the similar search of a Stregoni, and together we pursued this haunting idea and searched for a reliable House in Cuba. After some initial disappointment and discouragement initiation was obtained from two Paleros in the neighborhood of Pogolotti in La Habana. Rafael 'Felo' Reyes Cartas, a visionary artist and a painter of the nkisi living in modest surroundings was to be my godfather together with Pablo Perez. These men were a curious pairing. Felo was a man as equally occupied with Lucumi/Santeria as he was with Palo Maoymbe and regularly stressed the importance of godliness. Pablo on the other hand was a fierce anti-Christian, a quite hateful man who found enemies around every corner whom he sought to annihilate in whatever way possible. It was like being placed between God and the Devil – a union that at first seemed bizarre, but in time I realized that nothing could have been more perfect. Here I was, already at the beginning of my journey in Palo Mayombe scratched and forged in the very fiery centre that manifested the inherent tension and ambivalence of the cult. On my second visit to Cuba I was made Tata Nganga, which is what a priest of Palo Mayombe is called, and was given my Nganga in a double rama – or lineage. Felo was from Vence Batalla Vrillumba Viramundo and Pablo from Changani Brillumba Mayombe, a so-called ndoki rama. Later I was also received into the Kimbiza order which technically gives the foundation for a unique rama which I have given the name of Viramundo Brillumba Changani Kimbiza Vence Batalla. It is from this triple induction I am born and from this triple fire I write this book.

I believe my personal involvement together with my academic research in the field of Anthropology and the Science of Religion will enable me to provide a faithful living spiritual landscape of this Creole Sorcery. I will strive towards being truthful to the nature of the spirit retinue of the cult but also be sensitive to the reforms that took place on African soil in the 15th century as well as the Cuban contemporary conditions. As such I present this book as a gift to my nkisi, in honor of Nzambi and Lukankazi – and also as a memorandum for those Tata's and Yaya's that crossed my path, in whatever guise they chose.

Nsala Malecum!

Tata Remolino

I KALUNGA

THE VISIBLE & INVISIBLE HISTORY

History is commonly viewed as the gathering of events which occur across a horizontal line of time with a beginning and an end. But for the African mind, history is solely the repetition of timeless principles. Material history is followed as a bright shadow by the invisible powers that shape history. Therefore taking a purely materialist view of history when discussing African cultures will not produce a history which is truthful to the mindset and worldview of the participants of those particular events. Africans, as in all traditional cultures, tend to see history in the form of a circle and a cross. In other words, history is a repetition of eternal themes that occur in similar forms on a continuum of infinity. In this continuum the visible and invisible are at all times meeting and interacting, producing an alteration in the eternal continuum of repetition. This means that there is no act on earth that does not involve the invisible powers and there is no act happening now that is void of precedence in the past.

The history of Palo Mayombe starts with the presence and idea of *Kalunga*: the ocean, the means for the middle passage. For the inhabitants of the Central African coastline, the Kalunga was the passage to the kingdom of death and ancestry. The Kalunga was both a metaphor of death and the fluid immanence of death itself. The slave trade must also be viewed from this perspective, as the ebb and flow of Kalunga. At times the ocean was still yet soothing, at other times raging and violent. It was mystery and also a source for abundance symbolized by the fish. Humans were seen as not much different than the inhabitants of the ocean or the ocean itself. We are all beings composed of the same waters and like fish we adapt to the changes new waters offer. The Kalunga as carrier of ancestral memory created the perception of a shared materiality between the dead and the living under the collecting force of the One, *Nzambi*.

It seems that when it came to the idea of death the Ba'Kongo held a doctrine reminiscent of what we find in monothelitism, a doctrine concerning the dual nature of the savior. This doctrine, part of Christology, makes the argument that Jesus Christ simultaneously possessed a human and divine nature and that this dual nature was unified in one will. The monothelitist doctrine was abolished as a heresy by the Third Council of Constantinople in 680 when Pope Honorius suffered the accusation of heresy, claiming that the dual nature of the savior did not impair his will towards unification with the source. This again goes back to the early years of the Church and the Arian Controversy where the definition of the nature of Jesus Christ was of utmost importance. At the heart of the matter lies the debate concerning how we can know God – if at all – and to what extent creation carries witness to God or is divine in its own right. Any form of doctrine that was reminiscent of pantheism or animism tended to be viewed as an error. For instance it was the pantheistic error that was the final spark of fire which reduced the philosopher monk Giordano Bruno to ashes on the Inquisition's pyre in 1600. For the Christian missionaries the Kongo beliefs would be conceived as another form of this erroneous view.

This is suggested by using the allegory of the Kalunga as the manifestation of divine oneness and will shared by a dual substance, the dead and the living, which were believed to partake in a sameness separated by an invisible veil. This would be difficult to unite with accepted Christian doctrine in the Renaissance, which said quite the opposite and held a dualist stance concerning the living and the dead as well as the dual nature of the savior. Swirling under the Mission was the conflict between the monotheism of the Ba'Kongo and the binary theology of the Christians. At least this might be how Christianity appeared for the Ba'Kongo. Most curious of all to them was the Christian idea of the Devil who was presented as a diabolic enemy of God whilst being composed of the same superior substance as God, and seen as a negative embodiment of the divine. For the Ba'Kongo, Nzambi was the undisputed and all mysterious source of everything. Nzambi had no equal and thus concepts such as *mpemba* (the subterranean world) seem to have been slightly altered by the introduction of the diabolical.

The good/evil conflict presented in the form of God and Devil was to become a sad reality for the Ba'Kongo when the Portuguese arrived with gun and cross sanctioned by *the perfect prince*, João II (1455 – 1495). The nickname was given to him due to his perfection in replicating the regal model presented in Machiavelli's work *The Prince*.

When the Portuguese traveller and navigator Diogo Cão discovered the kingdom of Ba'Kongo in 1482, it was the riches along the Congo River that caused the greatest impression. Upon reporting his extraordinary findings Cão was commissioned by King João II to continue his journey down the African coast in search of the fabled Promised Land of Prester John, which was at the time believed to be India or perhaps Ethiopia. This legend is of great importance as it is here we find the impetus for the geographical explorations and discoveries in the Middle Ages and the Renaissance. It must have been a remarkable moment. The Portuguese had found the Promised Land and the Ba'Kongos at the shores of Loango and Luanda saw ancestors and spirits of death arriving across the Kalunga from the land of Death, their white skin testifying to this fact. It was a miraculous moment for Africans and Europeans alike. For some it was seen as a moment of meeting with the departed, for others a form of reaping, and for others it was a sign that the human journey was at an end and one would reunite with one's ancestors. No matter how they initially perceived the arrival of the Europeans a diverse range of perspectives on the white people and their faith was about to shape the history of Africa.

The Portuguese believed that the kingdom of Kongo was bigger than it actually was – compared to Iberia it was of truly amazing dimensions. They ended up loosely referring to the area from the south of Nigeria and to the north of the Kalahari Desert as Kongo and Angola due to linguistic similarities. This generalization lives on in Brazil where Kongo, Angola, Luanda and Arruanda often are lumped together in reference to the same illusory imperialist amalgamation of people. There were two main routes for the crossing of the Kalunga, one leading from the Kwanza river and to the port of Luanda and another leading from the Congo (now Zaïre) river to the hills of Mayombe and the city of Cabinda. These places were to become melting pots of Kongo religious diversity as they were important stations for the deportation of slaves. Here were found myths, legends and customs from all over the kingdom of Kongo which were to influence both South African and Caribbean faiths, religions and cults. It is most likely that here we find the cluster of ideas and practices in Candomblé, Umbanda, Kimbanda, Vodou and Palo Mayombe that are nominated as Kongo and Angola. Mayombe and Cabinda are important locations, but even more so was the island São Tomé (St. Thomas).

The first stop on the Trans-Atlantic trade route was the island São Tomé off the Nigerian coast. This island served both as a transit station as well as a massive sugar plantation in need of workers. When the Ba'Kongo ceased selling slaves in 1516 slaves were purchased and captured in other regions along the coast and over the next decade the numbers of slaves increased on the island leading to revolts, riots and a general increase in turbulence. Revolts took place with greater and greater aggression. Already in 1535 war camps composed of runaway slaves were becoming a real threat. These camps were alternatively referred to as *mocambos*, meaning sorrow, and *kimbundus*. We might see here a linguistic route of transmission into the use of mocambo or macumba in Brazil to describe the magical arts of the kimbundus, at times also written as Kimbunda and Kimbanda, the Brazilian cult of sorcery with the same name. By the same linguistic route the gathering of slaves from Cabinda and the Mayombe hills were transposed in Cuba as Palo Mayombe. From 1500 the slave trade from Central Africa transported the majority of slaves to Portugal, Spain and Brazil and the last great wave of Kongo migration to Cuba occurred from 1831 to 1867. This last wave is interesting as it was the last wave before slavery was abolished, partly due to greater and better organized kilombos and camps of renegade slaves across the Caribbean. This relationship with the war camps and revolt is significant for explaining the fiery and wild nature of Palo Mayombe as it throws light on the raw and dark flame of the Congo, Bizango and Petro rites in Haitian Vodoun. Naturally, Kongolese people had arrived in Cuba before the last wave – but this migration had an important and significant impact on the Cuban secret society, Abakuá and Palo Mayombe, through the work of Andres Petit.

The violent temper in the cult of Palo Mayombe is also traceable to the shift in African history marked by the arrival of the Europeans. Prior to their arrival the Kingdom of Ba'Kongo was more like a federation of clans and nations, an administrative unit ruled by a *manikongo*, the King of all Kongos. The manikongo reputed to have created this great gathering of nations and clans was the 12th century manikongo Nimi a Lukemi, who established his seat of power in the Crystal Mountains. The Ba'Kongos were renowned for their skills as metallurgists and weavers; they were described as a talented and sophisticated people that drew on a variety of skills. Infighting and warfare was always going on, but apparently not on the same scale as after the Europeans arrived. This important shift was in many ways instigated by Diogo Cão who on order of the King João II took four captives with him back to Portugal to educate them in European manners, imperialist thought and Christianity. In 1490 these four captives were returned to Kongo as a part of the mission. Gonçola de Sousa was appointed to lead the mission. Gonçola died in the crossing and his nephew Rui took over. With him came priests, soldiers and craft workers that would represent the superiority of European craftsmanship in masonry, artistry and weaving. At the same time he sent a mission of peace to Kongo King João II who was apparently also encouraging the feudal lords on São Tomé to ensure the development of criminal gangs on the island. In just a couple of decades São Tomé had become a festering hole of delinquents and criminals numbering several thousands of lawless people born from rape and prostitution. These 'Kimbanda mocambos' were then reintroduced into the kingdom of Ba'Kongo as a vile cancer to aid the Portuguese in destroying the kingdom. This was an incredibly devious plan; by reintroducing these corrupted people into the healthy Ba'Kongo kingdom they caused wars both within clans and between nations to escalate dramatically. Already in 1511 Nzinga Mbemba who was installed as the official Portuguese king of Kongo under the name of Alfonso I was writing letters to João II's successor, Manuel I (1469–1521) asking him to *subdue his ex-convicts*, but this response was just a sign that the plan had worked, thus more vandals were introduced to enhance the havoc. When João III (1502–1557) took the throne, the Luso-African trade, as they called it, was intensified. They plundered Ba'kongo for its vast riches, not only the natural resources, but also ivory, furs and of course people. Furthermore, as the kingdom disintegrated the Dutch, British and Belgians also became involved in Trans-Atlantic slavery leading to approximately 7 million Ba'Kongos being spread all over the Caribbean, Europe and Brazil in 300 years of slave trade. With the slaves' customs, belief, anger, fire and magic was made accessible outside of Africa and reshaped itself into the African Diaspora faiths, of which Palo Mayombe is one.

HEATHEN CHRISTIANITY AND AFRICAN TRADITION

When the Portuguese came to Kongo and Angola they were not only impressed with the extent of the Kongo kingdom, the richness of the culture and the production of fabric, crystals, sculptures and metals. They also found the manikongo himself to be impressive in his gentle ways and dazzling leadership qualities. Consequently it was crucial to convert the king. When the Portuguese arrived in 1490 the mission focused on converting the manikongo Nzinga a Nkuwu (reign from 1470 –1509). By 1491 Nzinga was baptized and appointed King of Kongo under the name of João I. Christianity was adopted both by him and his successors Alfonso I (Nzinga Mbemba) and Diogo I, (Nkumbi a Mpudi) and African aristocracy spread with the appointments of many dukes and counts between 1491 and 1561. This aristocratic class was by all measure Christian and received a good education. The missionaries hoped that by training an elite in the liberal arts and Christianity they could convert all the people. But Christianity was neither as peaceful an impulse as they hoped it would be – nor was it comprehended in the 'right' way. For instance, the half-brother of Alfonso I, Mpanzu a Kitima, opposed Christianity and wanted to uphold the traditional faith. Infighting grew in frequency and so did inter-state fights. Here we also find the many warrior societies entering the equation. Jaga, the warrior king of Kasanje might serve as an example, likewise the warrior clans in the Kingdom of Mutapa in the southern parts of Kongo. Here the

Muslims had a great influence and were unhappy with the Christian Mission, leading to what has been termed *the accidental crusade* in 1561 where Muslims, natives and the Portuguese were engaged in a confused fight, ending only with the retreat of the Portuguese due to fever and disease. Conversion turned out to be a frustrating affair which rather than uprooting their traditions gave an added dimension to the existing Kongo beliefs. After all, there were several factors in the Christian doctrine and its symbolism that would resonate with Kongo belief. The fact that the Kongo saw no contradiction in the dual observance of traditional faith and Christianity frustrated the missionaries to such an extent that they partly gave up on certain key concepts and allowed the heathen customs to be preserved, and partly gave up on these 'savages' altogether. Regarding the desire for conversion that took the form of Missions, this was certainly rooted in the problems the Church itself was faced with in the wake of the Reformation. From the 13th to the 16th century the papacy was beset with scandals from obscene behavior and practices, nepotism, through to the vulgar buying and selling of the throne of St. Peter. Something had to be done in order to restore the unity and purity of the Church. This state of heresy and fragmentation within the Church might have influenced the ways the missionaries decided to present the Gospel and also the level of intensity with which they imparted the Gospel. Not only this, but from 1536 the Holy See formally appointed King João III of Portugal as Inquisitor General as the Vatican's response to the increase in heresy.

John K. Thornton's research indicates the problem of establishing a coherent Central African cosmology, which makes it difficult to present an ethnography truthful to Kongo religion or belief as such. This is evident when we see the great differences between the Ki'Kongo speaking people in the larger parts of Ba'Kongo and the kimbundu speaking people mirrored against the mbundu speaking people towards the south eastern parts of the region. There were also several smaller clans and nations to the east and the south that the Kongo and Kimbundu referred to as *Nganguela* which was later equated with *mandingo* – both words carry the idea of something out of place, something strange and unclean that did not belong. Both words are found in present day Cuba

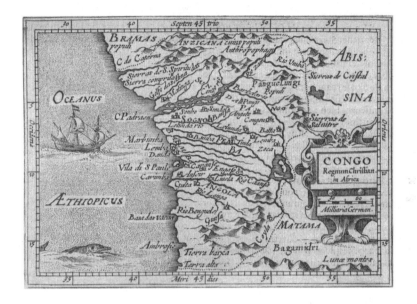

Map of the Kingdom of Kongo

in the cults of Palo Mayombe and the Cult of Osanyin. These parts, including Mbundu were virtually untouched by Christianity until the last great wave of enslavement in the middle of the 19th century. However, in spite of the problems with reconstructing a coherent belief system we can say that the cornerstone of the faith was rooted in revelation and precarious priesthoods. These priests or cult experts would be called *kimbanda* in the southern parts and *nganga* in the northern parts of what was invariably referred to as Kongo and Angola by the Europeans. Their sorcerous efficacy was demonstrated by their abilities as healers and mediums. This means that prophecy was essential to their religious expression and thus great differences would be found in definitions of purpose, hierarchy and ethos. A priest or leader for the cult was recognized by his skills in being an effective messenger for the invisible powers on the other side. This gave a great theological diversity that often confused and bewildered the Capuchin and Jesuit missionaries. Not only did they witness theological discrepancies from district to district, but due to the importance of ancestors matters could deviate even from family to family in the same village. The ancestral impulse reveals the traditional character of Kongo belief and it is therefore quite possible to present a coherent spiritual cosmology that reflects the traditional values inherent in Central African belief by focusing on key points in the region that made their way to the New World in the crossing of the Kalunga. Kongo faith might be described as an animist monism and it is in these waters that Kongo faith both meets and parts with Christianity.

The creative impulse, the One – *Nzambi Mpungu* – was seen as the aloof creator of the universe; at times he was considered the first ancestor, at other times as a genuine creative force it was possible to equate with the idea of a creator God. If Nzambi is viewed as the first ancestor the question of creation falls away and becomes redundant, and for many these forms of speculation were clearly nonsense as they had little practical use in daily life. To a larger extent it was an acceptance of the spiritual as a reality, of Nzambi and of the fluid immanence of one's ancestry. The mere fact that these ideas were accepted as undisputable truths contrasts with the modern mindset, one that was taking shape even in the 300 years of the Trans-Atlantic slave trade. This has created an even greater gulf between the Europeans and the Africans which we see today in much contemporary ethnography when it insists on understanding traditional non-western cultures on the basis of modern and western premises. This is akin to reading a book in a vaguely familiar yet still obscure language and guessing its meaning on the grounds of wanting knowledge of the language in question, and by filling in the gaps with social and personal experiences from one's own alien culture to understand the unknown other.

Nzambi and its plural form *jinzambis* seems to be understood as a creative and fertilizing agent. The movement itself, the fire is the active principle, it is what moves the Kalunga, the vastness. *Soba Kalunga* is the Lord of the underworld, but in reality, the underworld is not Kalunga, but *Ku'mpemba,** the world where the dead are living. This realm is guarded by *Luvemba*, meaning threshold or door, it is also known as *nsila*, a crossing or pathway. This world is often referred to as *ndoki*. Ndoki is a complicated term as today it is only used in reference to something evil or bad. In reality it is the knowledge from Ku'mpemba that we all bring with us and for some this can be strong, for others a weak knowledge. The Bwiti in Gabon refer to this portion of knowledge as coming with a shadow and the rites of Iboga initiation focus on removing the shadows we are born with and allowing the knowledge to flourish in a centered and benevolent manner that brings health to the society and the person in question. Ndoki is in other words a dark fire that often comes veiled in a particular negative pattern. But when encouraged to break out of its confinement this dark fire transforms into a great power for healing. Crucial here is the realization that ndoki is something we all have, in various degrees of occultation. Ndoki can also refer to ancestors, which is *Bakulu*, but a *Bakulu ndoki* would then be either a bad or a powerful (in the sense of a sorcerer) ancestor. The connotations of sorcery are correct, but we need to realize that sorcery is understood as a natural potency to cause transformation modeled

* This term lives on in Palo Mayombe under the name Kadiepemba, a name for the spirit of fire, often syncretized with the Devil or the mpungo Ndundu Karire, seen as the master of the crossing.

upon the action of fire. As with all things in nature it can strike to both sides, but it does possess an inherent tendency of pulling down and back energetically speaking. The idea of ndoki as reflected in the mystery of death and departed ones is reminiscent of the Greek concepts of *aōroi, biaiothanatoi* and *ataphoi,* those who died prematurely, violently or did not receive a proper burial ceremony. The good and the bad took part in a dynamic continuum, an ethical struggle that always sought equilibrium.

In Kimbundu-speaking areas the local deities had shrines, called *kiteki,* erected to them in high places, close to water or in wild territories, and especially in the *mbanzas,* the regional capital towns. Here the shrines could be quite elaborate and served as the devotional focus for the community. The Ndongo-speaking people arranged deities in pairs and families expressing a great awareness of the social role of the invisible powers. They also possessed a great awareness for *Kilundu,* which the Christians syncretized with the devil, as Kilundu was the one who gave prohibitions, formulated in the *kixila,* a set of negative and punitive laws. The Kilundu shrines were often placed in houses and frequently took a pyramidal shape, replicating the tripartite importance of existence. This might suggest a constant awareness of maintaining a high ethical standard as reflected in the form of oaths taken in the rites of passage focusing on the importance of being truthful and honorable. The Mbundus would at times build a pyramidal shape over the grave of their departed ones and set the pyramid with glass, so that the dead could have a window out on the world. Remnants of this are found in the diviners society, the Ngombo Nganga cult, and also in the mysterious *mpaka vititi* or *mpaka mensu* in Palo Mayombe. Household shrines, similar to the new world *bovedas* were also found where offerings of food and drink were placed out for the ancestors.

The kiteki of Kimbundu were in Loango called *nkisi* and the variety of deities worshipped changed according to regional needs and dispositions. An important deity for the Mayombe was called Maramba, represented by a beehive. Maramba served as the giver of good fortune in the hunt, fishing and health, but was also seen as stern in terms of oath. A taboo against lying was given to all young men initiated into it's cult as Maramba was the principal deity in the rites of passage to adulthood. This nkisi is similar to two other regional deities, the Chekoke of Loango and the Gumbiri at the port of Loango. These nkisis, or more correctly *minkisi* in its plural form, could vary greatly in appearance and shape, although the nkisis were most often gathered in large pots. The priests serving the nkisis or kiteki was called *nganga* or as in Kikongo, *nloko*, a reference which might be found surfacing linguistically in the importance of Lwa Loko in Vodou. We also find in the northern parts of Nsevo the shrine and cult of Nkita served by priesthood called *kitomi*, from where the Lemba and Nkita healing societies originated. Both in Cuba and Haiti they took the form of specific lineages or nations as well as spiritual qualities.

The term *nkisi* referred to a variety of manifestations, both as the spirit pot, a charm, a talisman, the person who held the power of the nkisi and so forth. Nkisi is often translated as medicine, which is a good term, if we focus on the holistic function of a medicine and not its material function of curing biological illness. Medicine seen as a spiritual agent that can improve conditions across a broad field would fit the idea of 'medicine' from an African perspective. In the areas that adopted Christianity the Church could also be called *nzo nkisi*, in the sense of Holy House or Holy point. The Kongo nkisi is unique in the African context as they are commonly equipped with nails and mirrors. The mirrors serve as windows for the soul of the nkisi and the nails are used to secure the spirit inside the vessel. The nkisi was a particular form of medicine, a holy medicine that both encapsulated a part of the divine, but was truly a living, divinely-endowed talisman. This was a god made by men, who were enabled to create by virtue of man being extensions of Nzambi on earth, thus creators by right. The nkisi was empowered by *bilongo*, the magical or active part of inspirited nature, such as herbs, animals and minerals. The bilongo was placed at the heart of the figure and animated. This would then constitute the soul-heart of the nkisi – and a mirror was placed over the bilongo so the heart could have eyes.

The nkisi, when endowed with the powers of bilongo, would then possess a number of powers and functions. The nkisi could be *nkondi* which could be used for harmful ends, like the *npezo* which also possessed a sinister reputation. *Na moganga* was a benevolent bilongo which protected against sickness and dangerous spirits and also served as a guide for hunters and warriors by giving them powers of astral travel and night-sight. The nkisi could also be *mbula* which protected against witchcraft and bad feelings directed towards a person or a city. All nkisi could be used for a variety of purposes but it was most important as a medicine that gave good fortune and dispelled bad things. The nkisi's ability to dispel was intimately tied in with the relationship it had with its owner, hence the word nkisi is often used interchangeably for the person possessing it and the nkisi itself.

In their work Wyatt MacGaffey and Robert Farris Thompson both focus on the *Yowa*, which is the Kongo cosmogram. This is essential to the understanding of Kongo belief and is found at the central and most important creative moment in Palo Mayombe as well. The simple structure of the Yowa replicates the Kongo worldview in such a way that its principles are replicated in all corners of the world in all scales. Thompson gives the following analysis:

> *The horizontal line divides the mountain of the living world from its mirrored counterpart in the kingdom of the dead. The mountain of the living is described as earth (ntoto). The mountain of the dead is called white clay (mpemba). The bottom half of the Kongo cosmogram was also called kalunga, referring, literally, to the world of the dead as complete (lunga) within itself and to the wholeness that comes to a person who understands the ways and powers of both worlds.*
>
> *Initiates read the cosmogram correctly, respecting its allusiveness. God is imagined at the top, the dead at the bottom, and water in between. The four disks at the points of the cross stand for the four moments of the sun, and the circumference of the cross the certainty of reincarnation: the especially righteous Kongo person will never be destroyed but will come back in the name or body of their progeny, or in the form of an everlasting pool, waterfall, stone or mountain.*
>
> *The summit of the pattern symbolizes not only noon but also maleness, north, and the peak of a person's strength on earth. Correspondingly, the bottom equals midnight, femaleness, south, the highest point of a person's otherworldly strength.*[†]

† Farris Thompson, Robert, *Flash of the Spirit*, p. 109.

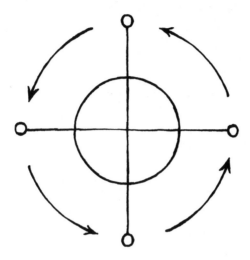

The Yowa, or Kongo Cosmogram

They recognized the Most High by their name: *Nzambi Mpunguin KiKongo*, who was the creator of all things. Nzambi was viewed as a remote force uninvolved with day-to-day human activity. The creation of nkisi would then reinforce and reconnect people with Nzambi through his many creative spirits. The fact that the Christian cross was so alike the Yowa enabled a unique and holistic view of Christianity as Nzambi had set his mark upon the faith. The cross simply delineated the upper human world from the lower ancestral world; as well as the female principle, at the left from the male principle on the right. As such the cross became a familiar symbol expressing the universal movement of all things.

What appears unique in the case of minkisi is how its very existence suggests man as creator. The nkisi is a wooden figure or an object filled with bilongo and animated by nature, the knowledge of its maker, the Nganga and Nzambi. The nkisi gives a materiality to the invisible powers oriented around a specific evil averting function. The skilled Nganga will be able to make a private or communitarian nkisi that resonates with the nature of the society where it is needed to execute its powers. It is common to equate the nkisi with Orisa, but this is not quite the case. The Orisa is more like the mpungo, one of Nzambi's divine rays. The nkisi on the other hand is something altogether different, the fruit of a dual creative process between the divine potency caught in matter and the mpungo who resonates with this potency. I believe this idea is demonstrated by the Kongo iconoclasm that repeatedly burst out. King Alfonso I in 1506 gathered enormous amounts of minkisi and burned them. In their ashes and embers were affixed crucifixes, crosses and saints. Counter-movements showed themselves of course, such as those of Queen Nzinga in the 16th century and later by Kimpa Vita, the prophetess in 1704 who burned crosses and saints and replaced them with minkisi. In addition we have the opinion of Kongo spirituality expressed by a great many Yoruba people which is that the Kongo are only *doing juju*. This might, as I understand it, be rooted in the active use of nkisi while the Yoruba is focusing on mpungo. The consequence of this is that the nkisi finds common ground with the god-making techniques in Aeschylus and thus is subject to a theological ambiguity that places it in the age-old Christian conflict between spiritual and demonic magic. The nkisi spans both sides of this division with one foot in mpemba and the other in Nzambi and unites left and right, the upper and the lower in conformity with the fundamental cosmological understanding of the Kongo consciousness.

These conclusions lead to yet another consideration that might present the nkisi in a very different light. If we look at Kongo history *the battle of the idols* began with Christianity. The missionaries went to heathen shrines and replaced what they found with crosses and saints. No matter what their motives were for doing this, the consequences were obvious – the nkisi became equated with saints. I believe this process expresses a deep truth, whether this was moved by an ignorance of the similarity between nkisi and saints or moved by the minkisi. Allow me to present a parallel approximation between nkisi and saints as it might have appeared for the Kongo:

Nkisi	Saint
Divine vehicle for Nzambi	Divine vehicle for God
Animated to life by divine creativity	Animated by God upon death
Worked by song and prayer	Worked by song and prayer
Material representation	Material representation
Prophetic	Prophetic
Holy/magical	Holy/magical

We should also keep in mind that in Cuba when they refer to *santo* or saint a similar process is taking place organically. The reference is to an Orisa, but a saint properly is a holy person who died and has been elevated. By applying the term saint to an Orisa the concept of nkisi is actually applied to the Orisa. Like the nkisi, the saint is in a unique position where they are both a divine messenger and a power that can help humans and inspire dreams and visions. For the Kongo these attributes were held both by the *bakulu*, ancestor, as well as the nkisi. Consequently, it means that syncretism between nkisi and orisa imparts an idea of holiness and divine connection that was very understandable for the Kongo and thus bridged the cultural division, but not necessarily in the way that the missionaries wanted. Through a gradual process of accepting and internalizing these ideas and propositions a greater understanding of the roots of Palo Mayombe and in particular the Kimbiza order will open up to you.

Ndozi is an important Kongo concept generally translated as dream, but seeing the great amount of uses this word is put to, it should be inferred that it is the multiple manifestations of dream awareness that we are speaking of. Nzambi, nkisi and mpungo speak in this state of altered and heightened awareness, which is the gate of vision, inspiration, dream, the prophetic and possession. It was here in the world of images that the powers of universal creativity descended like snakes coiling around the axis of the world making the world and all nkisi alive and vibrant. The dreaming awareness amongst the Kongo is similar to the one found in the Græco-Roman world. In the 19th book of Homer's *Odyssey* and likewise in Virgil's *Aenid*, dreams are located in the realm of Hades and can be either true or false. Penelope dreams of two doors, the ivory gate of false dreams and the horned one of true dreams. Both doors allow dreams to pass through into the world of the living, to deceive or enlighten, to give rise to flights of fantasy or flights of imagination. The Kongo likely perceived dreams as spectres and ghosts and thus approached dreams as they did messages from the ancestors. For the Christians this generated anxiety as shown in the dream of Saint Jerome. The pagan inheritance Christianity tried to reform or rewrite or reinterpret throughout the Middle Ages surfaced again when they were confronted with Kongo beliefs.

Imagination and dream was not a foreign concept for medieval man. It was the power of imagination that drove the Europeans in search of HyBrazil, Pindorama and Eldorado. Exploration fueled by imagination began quite early, perhaps around the 8th century, but increased in vigor from the 12th century with the great popularity of the famous text *Legenda Aurea*, or *Golden Legends of the Saints' Lives* published in 1260. An important nucleus of these legends was the concept of fantastic and faraway kingdoms representing the Golden Age. It is here we find the legendary kingdom of Prester John. The title *Prester* is derived from the French *prêtre*, meaning both priest and king – in the manner of the biblical Melchizedek. Prester John was a mythical medieval emperor whose kingdom was believed to extend from Babylon to India. Both these region were under the rulership of Alexander the Great (356–323 BCE) and several mythical kingdoms were ascribed to this enigmatic emperor. Some said he was descended from the Three Magi or Melchizedek himself, others that he was descended from St. Thomas, the apostle of doubt. The island São Tomé was named after the apostle Thomas and this reveals the importance of the legend of Prester John for the explorers.

The first mention of Prester John is found in the *Chronicle of Otto*, or more formally, *Chronica sive Historia de duabus civitatibus* penned by the Bishop of Freising in 1145. It was this text in particular that inspired the explorers, and especially the sea-faring Portuguese. In fact,

the Portuguese held on to this legend until the end of the 17th century
and several of the explorers were given royal letters which they should
give to Prester John if they met with him. Since Prester John's kingdom
was described as heathen, both conversion and plunder were the motive and ambition of these explorations. His land was rich in silver, gold
and all precious stones and he himself was said to carry a sceptre made
of pure emeralds. Many fantastic things were found in Prester John's
paradisiacal lands. Here grew the wonderful plant Assidos which, when
worn by anyone, would not only protect them from any evil spirits but
would also allow them to command them. It was further believed that
his empire contained a fountain of youth and that he ruled with the aid
of a magic mirror in which he could see everything that was happening
in all provinces of his empire.

In 1165 a letter fell in the hands of the Byzantine emperor Manuel I
Comnenus, allegedly from Prester John. Some parts of this letter might
reveal why the fascination for finding this kingdom grew to such dimensions in Europe.

*Our land is the home of elephants, dromedaries, camels, crocodiles, meta-
collinarum, cametennus, tensevetes, wild asses, white and red lions, white
bears, white merules, crickets, griffins, tigers, lamias, hyenas, wild horses,
wild oxen, and wild men — men with horns, one-eyed men, men with eyes
before and behind, centaurs, fauns, satyrs, pygmies, forty-ell high giants,
Cyclopes, and similar women. It is the home, too, of the phoenix and of
nearly all living animals.*

*We have some people subject to us who feed on the flesh of men and of
prematurely born animals, and who never fear death. When any of these
people die, their friends and relations eat him ravenously, for they regard
it as a main duty to munch human flesh. Their names are Gog, Magog,
Anie, Agit, Azenach, Fommeperi, Befari, Conei-Samante, Agrimandri,
Vintefolei, Casbei, and Alanei. These and similar nations were shut in
behind lofty mountains by Alexander the Great, towards the north. We
lead them at our pleasure against our foes, and neither man nor beast is left
undevoured, if our Majesty gives the requisite permission. And when all
our foes are eaten, then we return with our hosts home again.*

The Kingdom of Prester John

These accursed fifteen [twelve?] nations will burst forth from the four quarters of the earth at the end of the world, in the times of the Antichrist, and overrun all the abodes of the saints as well as the great city Rome, which, by the way, we are prepared to give to our son who will be born, along with all Italy, Germany, the two Gauls, Britain, and Scotland. We shall also give him Spain and all of the land as far as the icy sea. The nations to which I have alluded, according to the words of the prophet, shall not stand in the judgement on account of their offensive practices, but will be consumed to ashes by a fire which will fall on them from heaven.

Our land streams with honey and is overflowing with milk. In one region grows no poisonous herd, nor does a querulous frog ever quack in it; no scorpion exists, nor does the serpent glide amongst the grass, not can any poisonous animals exist in it or injure anyone.

Anthropologists in the 19th century claimed that the African culture was full of primitive superstition, but as this little excerpt from Prester John's letter shows, the imagination of Europe was equally fertile and fantastic in the age of exploration. Since this account at least indirectly motivated the Trans Atlantic exploration, it is fair to say that for the missionaries it was not a meeting with superstition that occurred in Kongo, but more a confrontation of the spiritual and pure against the dark and demonic. It was false dreams meeting true dreams so to speak. Considering that the Kongo had already adopted Christianity in 1491 it would indicate that common theological ground was found. Seeing the iconoclasm occurring some 15 years later, this would further indicate that the conversion took a real hold on influential people in the community and thus made an impact on wider society.

There were several theological principles the Christians brought that the Kongo resonated with. The rituals of baptism as a way of receiving the Holy Spirit and the purifying effects of blessed water would have been known to them. Considering the use of cold water as a medium for the appeasement of spirits in Kongo – as in most parts of West Africa – it was no mystery that baptism would possess great purifying and magical qualities. Consequently they gravitated towards this already familiar ritual element. The cross was another familiar icon associated with Nzambi's positive presence in the world and the crucifixes were representatives for minkisi.

Other factors that would resonate were the stories of creation, the genesis, which presented God in a creative way that was reminiscent of Nzambi. This association was even reinforced by the missionaries who at times named Kongo Churches as Munanso Nzambi, House of Nzambi. The harmonious equation of God and Nzambi was agreed upon to a great extent, so naturally, the creative potential of the Supreme God was not up for debate. Rather it was the 'theological error' of the Kongo that gave cause for concern. The mystery of the mass, which animated and transformed bread and wine into living sacraments was a mystery not much different from making nkisi. The invisible domains were another area of agreement – and in the end if you called angels for mpungo or the saints for nkisi the difference was not necessarily a cosmological one, but a theological one. There were many factors that did not present any theological friction for the existing Kongo belief in the Kongolese perception of Christianity. Even the socially regulating codes found in Kongo society, the kixila laws, with their punitive character, had much in common with Christian morality and ethics.

Besides 'pagan perspectives' upon the Christian mystery and the refusal of the Africans to give up polygamy, the greatest point of divergence concerned the dead and ancestry. The Church had since the 7th century, as a consequence of the decisions made at the Third Council of Constantinople in 680, dealt a damaging blow to the sanctity of ancestry. Since the 7th century it was forbidden to bury loved ones in the soil of their home. Instead the Church was on an ever greater scale providing graveyards for this purpose. Under ecclesiastical jurisdiction the rich were accommodated in mausoleums and remembered, whilst the common people were placed in mass graves and the bones later exhumed to furnish ossuaries or bone chapels. In this way they eradicated the sense of ancestry which the Africans refused to let go of. They knew that without the support of ones ancestors they would be nothing and soon forgotten. The ancestors represented the accumulated wisdom of generations – and also, the dead were never considered to be dead, rather they were the *not-living* who continued to exert an influence from the other side of the veil.

KONGO COSMOLOGY AND HERACLITUS' FLUX & FIRE PHILOSOPHY

It might seen strange to bring in the works of Heraclitus in this context, but this is perhaps less strange than the similarities of metaphysical ideas expressed by this Greek thinker and the dynamics in Kongo expressions of the dialectics of their cosmology. Dr. Fu-Kiau, who was an important informant for Farris Thompson, attempts to present what he understands to be the general Kongo idea of cosmos and creation. His focus is particularly on the Bantu speaking Kongos, which counts Kimbundu, Umbundu, Ki-Kongo and more than 500 other languages defined within the same linguistic group. So, it is a large and ambitious canvas which he works with to both explain and illustrate the inherent unity of their ideas. He envisions the primordial state of the world to be a vast nothingness composed of active, yet unmanifest potencies. The potency of fire started to move the nothingness and generated Kalunga. All stellar bodies were then born from this movement of fire in the emptiness and the *flux and fire* of creation became the principle for change, force and vitality – the Kalunga. As the stellar bodies cooled down the process of cooling itself produced waters and from this rivers, oceans and mountains. The *nza*, or the world, was born by the powers of Nzambi and points of power on earth were therefore called *nzo*, the world, as a reference to Nzambi manifest in a particular location. The Kalunga then became synonymous with change, space, the movement of the ocean and Nzambi the creative force that sculpts these masses and potencies became more associated with dough, dampness and the waters. So, we have here three principles that are replicated at all times in the nza, they are expansion, contraction and movement, this is replicated at all times in birth, death and the movement that is always occurring. It happens when the sun rises and the moon rises and all movements between daybreak and dawn. This triad is symbolized by three fire stones, the basic element of creation. The importance of these three stones of fire and thunder is replicated in the social structure just as it is in the spiritual structure of both Central Africa and Cuba.

The 4th century BCE Greek philosopher Heraclitus held similar views of creation and it is also interesting to take note of the similarities between the Kongo warrior ethos and the ethos propagated by Heraclitus. It has been suggested that Heraclitus' intense misanthropy caused him to see war and death as nothing more than what mankind is due, and given their immense stupidity well deserved. His exaltation of war, as the mother of all things, emerges naturally from his philosophical fragments. That he was not particular positive towards humankind is clear from his general debunking of all other philosophers and his admonition to the people of Ephesus, his hometown, that they should all hang themselves. Prior to Heraclitus, the general focus of philosophy concerned the essence and stability of things. When Heraclitus enters the scene and says: *You cannot step into the same river twice, for fresh waters are ever flowing in upon you,* he is actually presenting a perspective that is radically different from the ethereal speculations and truths of his time, a position which caused him to frown upon the views of his contemporaries. He held that everything was in flux, change and transition at all times. As he said: *There is exchange of all things for fire and of fire for all things, as there is of wares for gold and of gold for wares.*

Heraclitus held that fire is the primordial element out of which everything else arises. Fire is the origin of all matter; through it things come into being and pass away. Fire itself is the symbol of perpetual change because it transforms a substance into another substance without being a substance itself: *This world, which is the same for all, no one of gods or men has made; but it was ever, is now, and ever shall be eternal fire;* and: *Fire lives the death of air, and air lives the death of fire; water lives the death of earth, earth that of water.* Heraclitus thinks of fire not as destructive but merely a transforming power. The process of transformation does not happen by chance, but is, according to Heraclitus, the product of God's reason – *logos* – which is identical with the cosmic principles. He sees that God is living in every soul and in every material thing on earth. The fiery element is the expression of God in everything, thus he is in every sense a pantheist. This universe, which is the same for all, has not been made by any god or man, but it always has been, is and will be, an ever-living fire, kindling itself by regular measures and going out by regular measures.

Another of Heraclitus' main teachings can be called the *unity of opposites*. The unity of opposites means that opposites cannot exist without each other – there is no day without night, no summer without winter, no warm without cold, no good without bad. To put it in his own words: *It is wise to agree that all things are one. In differing it agrees with itself, a backward-turning connection, like that of a bow and a lyre. The path up and down is one and the same.* From a modern perspective it seems trite to state that opposites are the same, yet to the Greek it was not entirely obvious. Hot and cold could both be expressed as degrees of temperature and dark and bright as degrees of light. Nonetheless, the Heraclitean theory of perpetual flux and universal transformation goes far beyond what was obvious to the ancients and finds resonance with the Kongolese world view in the Middle Ages. The idea of flux and fire is also found today as a fundamental principle in Palo Mayombe. Kalunga is the flux and it is this flux that is the life giving powers in the nganga. The fire as manifest in conflict, killing, fire itself and the essential nature of the thunderstone is the breath of life to the nganga. It is from this continuous interaction between fire and water that change and transformation is accomplished, and it is this perception that underlies Heraclitus' proposition of war as the natural condition in a world fluid with fire, *that strife is justice, and that all things come to pass through the compulsion of strife.* In Palo Mayombe this flux and fire element is constantly present, from the basic methods of bilongo and nkisi construction to the social interactions. Of interest here is what is known as lengua. Lengua is the ritual code of proverbs in Palo Mayombe. Lengua is exercised in puyas or verbal contests, a tug of war between two paleros where knowledge is exchanged in coded ways to demonstrate superiority. By doing this they replicate the flux of Kalunga by using verbal sparks of fire, thus generating movement on various levels depending on the context.

To arrive at the centre of the mystery of Palo Mayombe we need to go outside the formal cosmology of Kongo spirituality which centred around the king and his diviners. The Kongo and neighboring lands were reputed for their strong warrior societies and I believe we need to factor these clans and societies in Palo Mayombe's origin. The origins are of course a composite of various African and Christian factions fused again during the Diaspora. The nganga, also called *prenda* in Cuba, are understood slightly differently based on what rama or lineage we are considering. When it comes to the prendas nominated as ndoki or pure Mayombe their origin might be located in the sorcerous activities of the warrior clans who waged wars repeatedly on Muslims. At least this would contribute to an explanation of the use of the traditional Arabic greeting, *Nsala malecum*, being used as a greeting amongst paleros and also as a greeting of the prenda.

As demonstrated in the historical recapitulation the vast district referred to as 'Kongo' was composed of a host of nations where war was a constant factor. It was a field of fire and blood. This nerve of fire is present in Palo Mayombe today as all paleros consider themselves as born by fire – and many see the medium of birth as the gate of death. By the creed you live, you shall also perish. There is one 'Kongolese' district in particular which is interesting to consider as a likely origin of the Paleros prenda or nganga, namely Kasanje, the kingdom of fierce and often anti-Christian manikongos, such as those of Jaga and the Imbangala people. The origin of the Imbangala is unclear and attempts to assimilate them with and differentiate them from the Jagas has so far been unsuccessful though this is not of great importance for this treatise. Both the Jaga and in particular the Imbangala had a dark reputation. There were also further north an Akan related people who were said to file their teeth sharp so they could with greater ease consume their enemies. These are only two peoples renowned for their cannibalism and antinomian practices. The Imbangala were usually depicted as vandals with no respect for any living thing, including nature. Instead of regularly tapping the palm-trees for wine, they cut them down and dried them out. Instead of planting vegetables themselves they stole somebody elses. They delighted in usurping and defiling other people's labor and values. They were considered a highly predatory warrior clan. In times of dire need their expertise would be sought by Kongo chieftains and their aid was also procured by the Portuguese.

The Imbangala were most likely a foreign people that moved into Kongo from the south. Gilberto Freyre and Leo Frobenius in their ethnography describe how they discovered in the south-eastern parts of Kongo a people who spoke a language borrowing much from Fanti and Kwa. Their language, music, clothes, agricultural ideas and cult bore much similarity with the Arabic Almoravid people. The likely assumption is that these people were driven to this part of Kongo around 1070 when the Almoravid entered into war with the Akan people of lower Ghana, most likely motivated by taking over the fertile area around Lake Chad where the Akan people lived. This was a war with no winners and led to Kwa and Fanti speaking people being spread to further parts of Kongo. It has been suggested by John Coleman De Graff Johnson, that there is a connection with the Munango warriors of Kasangu, based on similarities of language, dress and customs. The Munangos were a warrior society, again noted for their habit of filing their teeth sharp. Their function was to defend the king and they lived in a strict matrilineal society where women were in control. Charles Beadle in his rather exalted account, *Witch Doctors*, tells how this warrior society in the 16th century sunk into decay with one of the clan leaders challenging the matrilineal rulership by rape, abduction of women and starting a war spree in the village of Kalamba in Kongo (present day Zaïre). The timeline he suggests fits quite well with the introduction of the delinquents from São Tomé being unleashed on Kongo as well as the counter revolts against the Christians by the anti-Christian Imbangala warriors. I believe it is partly from these warrior societies we can trace the origin, cosmology and technology of how the nganga of Palo Mayombe is made. I believe it is from these societies we find the origin of animating non ancestral bones and greetings such as *nsala malecum* in Palo Mayombe.

The term *nganga* is in use in several Central African districts and kingdoms as a reference to a sorcerer or a healer and as is common in most African languages the object and its owner are usually not seen as distinct from each other. A word like nganga could refer to both the practitioner and the tools of his practice; the prenda of the Palero which is the cauldron of terracotta or iron that holds the secrets of the nganga. The main secret is twofold, first it is the heart of the prenda and then the *nfuri* or *nfumbe* which is manifested by the presence of human bones. Nfuri and nfumbe is today used interchangeably for the bones, but some make a distinction between nfuri being *agitated* or *vile* bones and nfumbe those of a more cooperative nature.

The prenda is a cauldron composed of human bones, dirt and sticks. This could be done with ones ancestors or fellow tribesmen in order to facilitate a stronger spirit presence by cementing their powers in such a way. There is however a difference in applying this technology with the bones of your enemy or simply non ancestral bones. The idea of placing the bones in a cauldron and igniting them with life with the purpose of bringing them into being as a slave is an attitude held by quite a few paleros. This attitude reminds us in ethos of the creed of the Imbangala warriors who would seek to reanimate fallen enemies as their servants.

Elements of Imbangala rituals were cannibalistic and cruel. For instance the Ndongo Queen Njinga went to a clan of Imbangala living in a kilombo in Matamba in 1629 with the intention of gathering a band of Imbangala warriors to fight the white usurpers. It is said that her initiation as a warrior queen involved crushing and pounding a baby in a mortar and consuming it. The Imbangala inducted their captives into clanship in cruel and vile ways. Since they refused to let their own women give birth the growth of the tribe was accomplished by taking captives and using foreign women as hosts for their offspring. The captives went through a ruthless training and were not admitted into the clan before they had successfully killed and consumed an enemy in combat. This marked a turning point where they were considered Imbangala. The warrior code of the Imbangala was rooted in a particular understanding of the kixila law and a great focus on the abduction not only of enemies, but also of the spiritual and magical powers they might possess or be in touch with. This led to defamatory acts being used as sorcerous strategies against both Muslims and Christians as well as their holy objects and relics. By dethroning and overcoming an enemy and stealing his sacred objects and words of power the warrior would takeover the enemy both spiritually and as an ancestor. An Imbangala warrior could for instance slaughter a missionary, eat his body and his bible, turn his bones into a nkisi and salute him with *Amen* as a way of absorbing the power. In the same way it is not difficult to envision how the Imbangala warrior upon slaughtering a Muslim could have placed his head (the seat of the soul) into a vessel, creating a nkisi saluting the vessel with his own sacred words, *salaam-walekum*. The Palo Mayombe greeting *Nsala malecum* might be a faint memory of its origins amongst the sorcerous and antinomian warrior clans of Central Africa.

The cult of healers and diviners, such as the Nkita and the Lemba of Calabar also influenced Palo Mayombe, but it seems to a lesser degree than the impact these cults had on Vodou in Haiti – and of those in particular the Nkita society. The *mpaka mensu*, the diviners horn and the oracles of four, seven, nine or sixteen configurations made visible by throwing divinatory objects made part of the secrets of these societies. Parts of these cults entered Cuba and took root in Palo Mayombe, but apparently without a significant enough number of members from these societies to sustain the original cults. Still, 'the diviners' horn' and the different oracles using cowry, coconut or bone are the heritage Palo Mayombe preserved from these cults and perhaps also the herbal lore, yet without much direct reference back to these societies. As such, Palo Mayombe is a sorcerous synthesis of a rich African legacy veiled in its present Creole form.

PALO MAYOMBE COSMOLOGY

*He who swears to God has also sworn to the Devil**

There is no devil per se in Palo Mayombe, but a cosmic antagonism that unfolds in war and agitation as the energy behind movement. These are the two faces of Nzambi, his night and his day. You cannot have the day without the night and otherness is always around us, like an invisible mirror leading to the land of death and ancestry. It is this metaphysical principle that is the taproot of Palo Mayombe. This binary pull within Nzambi also carries the historical memory of a heritage torn ruthlessly between the material and the spiritual, effectuating its mutual benefit and its innate harmony. Given the cruel history of Palo Mayombe it is amazing to see how this movement towards unity and connectedness is still at work. Even if much oral lore has been turned into silence during the crossing, the cultural ambivalence from Kongo and Angola has served as a flame of continuation and truthful adaptation to a new land. After all the land, the *ntoto*, is the field of definition and as such Palo Mayombe has stayed true to its roots.

The perceived dualities in Palo Mayombe are always reflections of the same cycle, as night is to day and day is to night. *Nkuyu* is ancestry useful and fertile, under the domain of light – *ndoki* is ancestry, but the veiled parts, the night of the ancestors. We all carry these elements within us; they are parts of our unique composition and define our actions. When we transgress and commit violence or miracles we express ndoki, the powerful part of ourselves that remains hidden from light. This can serve for good or ill depending on the social context and the degree of wisdom we exercise.

In contemporary Palo Mayombe a tension bordering on dualism is found in the relationship between Nzambi and Lukankazi. Nzambi is viewed as God while Lukankazi is viewed as the Devil. Amongst the

* Palo proverb.

Bakongo, Nzambi was the omnipotent who revealed himself in nature and the wood clad mountains in particular, hence the denomination *Palo* – sticks from the kingdom of Nzambi. Lukankazi on the other hand was a *mpungo* of the sky and, given his association with fire, most likely related to the thunderstone and lightning. As such, Lukankazi was in a way the God of night, while Nzambi represented all beauty and fertility under the Sun. Again, the dyadic relationship is not a dualism as such, but a recognition that change brings different types of potencies to the forefront of existence. It is not about a hierarchy but about realizing what force rules specific powers and times – all under the auguries of Nzambi. In this light we find a most interesting historical event that might have affected the later development of Christian and Jewish prendas. The latter understood to be related to Lukankazi, the spirit of fire and hence ndoki in the sense of being evil, like the devil, replicating the Imbangala attitude towards the Christians. This African conflict has its mirror image in Europe which might explain the introduction of Jewish as synonymous with bad, and also illuminate the Arabic greeting *Nsala Malecum* used in Palo Mayombe from yet another angle. Considering the historical timeline it is worth noting the temporary unification of the Iberian kingdoms of Castile and Aragon in 1496 by Isabella of Castile and Ferdinand of Aragon. This unification was the result of unruly decades beginning with the Moorish invasion in 1002 and finally finding peace under Catholic reign in 1474 when Isabella the Catholic was appointed queen of Castile. A similar succession happened in Aragon until Ferdinand the Catholic married Isabella. In this time frame we also have the Black Death which raged though Europe from 1348 until early 19th century. Iberia was first confronted with the Muslim invasion and then the 'Jewish curse' of the plague – both being equated with something nasty, bad, evil (that is, *ndoki*) – a nightly fire out of control. Either by their blackened skin or blackened with disease, these were denizens of the evil night. As such the denomination of unholy prendas being called Jewish could be traced back to these dramatic transformations on the Iberian Peninsula and thus become equated with witchcraft in its worst sense. If this is so, the missionaries managed to colour the Kongo inspired faiths in such a way that Christianity can be understood to be the primordial syncretism and thus an avenue of understanding more true to the core of Kongo spirituality than the later Yoruba syncretism that happened in the New World. It is my understanding that in terms of the Kongo Mission we are speaking of a synthesis more than a syncretism. The central African people were taught the ways of Christianity and only permitted a merging where precedence was already established in the spiritual order of Nzambi. This attitude is upheld in the Kimbiza rama, both the ancient one and the lineage reformed by Andres Petit.

In contemporary Palo Mayombe it is common to use syncretism more than synthesis. This syncretism is by way of the Yoruba vinculum where the nature of *orisa* is used to explain mpungo and nkisi. Both orisa and mpungo manifest as natural phenomena, so there is no discrepancy in equating the mpungo Nsasi and the orisa Sango with thunder. The problem enters when the stories of orisa becomes the stories of mpungo. The fact that two spirits share the same natural power does not imply a direct fusion. Here enters the ancestral element as defined by culture and heritage. This is further complicated by the differences in spiritual technology between the Yoruba and the Kongo and even more so by the prejudice the Yoruba hold when speaking of their neighbors. This is largely motivated by the complexity of Yoruba metaphysics mirrored against the practical aspirations of the Kongo people. Considering the distance both social and spiritual between Yoruba people and Kongo people, the Christian syncretism is actually more true to the nature of Palo Mayombe than the borrowings from Yoruba derived Santeria and Lucumi. I am of the opinion that this syncretism in a Creole faith is understandable and workable, but nevertheless misleading and ultimately unnecessary.

Over the last two decades or so Santeria has been referred to as Magical Catholicism by practitioners and anthropologists and this does reflect both a meeting and a departure point in the general Creole spirituality. Still, the idea of nkisi and the nganga is a wholly Kongo concept and its mirror in Yorubaland, namely the *Shigidi*, did not make part of the Santeria equation on traditional premises. This means that whatever approximations can be drawn between mpungos and orisas they are missing out on important distinctions defined by ancestry and lineage.

It is perhaps possible to trace the syncretic factor to the term *Creole*. When the Portuguese – and by extension the Spaniards – arrived in Kongo they had offspring that were neither European nor African and thus entered into a middle-class able to draw on both heritages. This is attested to by the use of *criollo* as a term designating this middle ground in the Iberian perception of caste. It also clearly shows the low opinion the explorers held of the Africans as it was believed that the European blood elevated the offspring to a state of limbo between the African and European. We shall not enter here into the Iberian concepts of cleanliness of blood but just state that the consequence of this was an amazing opportunity of being subject to a dual heritage that potentially could enrich the individual. With the entrance of the spirit of modernity and its obsession of defining *what is* in terms of *what it is not* the criollo ended up between two poles and their potential as a bridge was replaced with syncretism. Here we find an important anxiety and social tension that few people today dare venture into, fraught as it is with prejudice and racism. The whole issue is rooted in a disintegration of tradition replaced with a profane taxonomy that whilst obsessed with category does not understand the composite.

Palo Mayombe is a cult subject to a great variety of distinctions and explanations in terms of origin and nature. This is caused partly by syncretism, both religious and social but also the forgetting of ones roots, which often happens when a tradition adapts itself to a new land. This forgetfulness can be a good thing, but depending on the social context it can also introduce much bias and distortion.

Syncretism always speaks of the play between power and resistance in a culture. This interaction based on a nerve of fire shows itself in the African Mission. In large parts of Ewe and Bantu speaking parts of Africa it was crucial to elect a reference to God and another reference to take the place of the Devil. As such the traditional monism of the Africans was subject to the forces of distortion already in Africa and this naturally continued and gave birth to a binary world view at times adopted by practitioners of African inspired cults in the New World by the mere presence of an adversary. In spite of this, the original monism speaks quietly in proverbs and tales erasing duality in favor of a harmonious cosmology situated around an owner of heaven, earth and creation.

The houses, *munansos,* and the lineages, *ramas,* do possess some variations that give rise to disputes over superiority. This is most evident in *langue* which occurs at times when paleros meet. Langue takes the form of a battle of wisdom, where proverbs, *mambos* (songs) and fragments of myths, usually of a Kikongo derivation, are used in a battle between the paleros. The inherent tension in Kongo ancestry itself continues through this practice which for an outsider can appear to be a form of public debunking of each other.

It is popularly accepted that the impulses that were to generate Palo Mayombe arrived in Cuba in the 16th century, brought by Kongolese slaves of royal descent. At least this is the common myth informing the cult's origin. It is quite likely that the cults taking shape into Palo Mayombe consisted of highly secretive and selective groups guarding a nganga. This would be even more reasonable seeing that until the middle of the 19th century Palo was largely barred to Caucasians and likewise the secret society Abakuá, derived from the leopard societies in Central Africa. The entrance of Creole and white was opened by a Haitian Creole Andrés Facundo de los Dolores Petit, himself a Mason and a man of mixed blood. Through his affiliation with one of the two fundamental and traditional Abakuá societies he created the Kimbisa Order, or rather, in full, Orden Kimbisa del Santo Christo el Buen Viaje. This was the beginning of Creole Palo. This means that it was Andres Petit who opened the doors to the Creole sorcery of Palo Mayombe. With the opening of the doors a great syncretism occurred and an equally great diversity in opinions.

Given the focus Palo Mayombe has on death and sorcery, it has gained a heavy reputation for being a portal for vile and sinister magic of the blackest kind. This has led some to make distinctions between *paleros* being bad and *mayomberos* being good. Here we find the imposed dualism between Nzambi and Lukankazi at play: those who work the garden of Nzambi (paleros) being good, but the others being bad. The *ngangualeiro* (holder of Nganga/priest) who sees nature as superior to man, which contains a lack of respect for the human soul, is by virtue sinister – and when this is reversed we find the benevolent reflection of the white sorcerer who works in service for human kind. The same contrast is found in the distinction between a baptized or Christian prenda/nganga and a ndoki or *judia* (Jewish) prenda/nganga: the latter designates a prenda that is made to work for evil, while the baptized prenda works for good. The prenda or nganga is your foundation. The Nganga is in Cuba the name for the spirit vessel itself, while in Congo the word refers to the sorcerer. They are both right, because in reality there is no distinction between the potency of the Nganga and the holder of the vessel. A pact is made to align the *nfumbe* or *nfuri* with the Tata Nganga.

It is a common belief that this duality is a result of syncretism on one hand and a way of masking pagan beliefs behind Christian saints on the other. Following this thread of reasoning Andres Petit is commonly seen as an innovator of a particular fusion of Congolese and Christian theology. This is most likely not the case. I believe Andres Petit actually made accessible a 'Congolese' spirituality that was pretty much intact since the 17th century amongst the loose cabildos in Cuba, whereas some formed into Abakuá societies with the arrival of Masonry. This idea suggests itself when we apply historical scrutiny and discernment; it is obvious that many slaves in the crossing were already Christian. Of course not all adopted the new faith and here we perhaps find the hard distinction between good and evil along very Christian lines.

The connection with Abakuá societies is implied by the name Mayombe itself, a specific area in the upper Congo where the Carabali's came from. The name referred to the cross river region of Calabar, between upper Kongo and Lower Nigeria that served as a slave port. From here they were taken to the city of Regla, which nowadays makes up one of the neighborhoods in Havana. This was the last big wave of slaves that began in 1836. From this wave grew the secret society of Abakuá, a continuation of the leopard societies of the Efik and Ejagham people. The society was similar to Masonry and was strict and orderly. They had much in common with Palo Mayombe, but seem to have managed to secure a more stringent corpus of lore and complexity – at least if the *anaforuana*, the Abakuá firmas are taken into consideration. In these designs we find a greater array of themes and complex mysteries expressed. Likewise in their well organized theatrical dance dramas they perform further complexity is found. These dancers are called *ñañigos* or *ireme*, or just as commonly, *diablitos* (devils). They dress in a checkerboard costume which is reminiscent of the vestment of the members of the leopard cult. The specific design also brings to our attention the Yoruba's neighboring Calabar with their Ogboni society – they have an important relationship to the leopard and serve as the council of elders with some Masonic similarities. The conical rag used to cover the head completes a costume that actually reminds us of the Egungun cults amongst the Yoruba. Seeing that the Abakuá's most important day is Twelfth Night, the 6th of January – a day of misrule and the three magi – and how they unleash the diablitos upon the streets to honour the presence of the other world amongst us, there is clearly a vibrant ancestor cult burning at its foundation. I believe the arrival of the Abakuá in many ways sustained Kongo sorcery and was instrumental in Palo Mayombe managing to preserve its authentic flavor. This would also be suggested by the large amount of paleros who are member of the Abakuá society.

This most benevolent influence aside, a certain deconstruction of Bantu culture through migration and social influences did take place. This generated some divergence in doctrine and dogma from the original, and out of a neo-construction born from fragmented tradition and social pressure the cult takes form. Its rich origins are to some extent visible in the diversity of house customs and variations in terminology. It might be that the cult itself went through a similar process as we see the language went through. The Bantu and Ewe dialects from Congo and Angola degenerated in Cuba, leading to a variation in pronunciation and meaning that gradually dislocated the emerging Palo Mayombe cult from the metaphysical principles of its origins.

ON THE POSSESSION OF SPIRIT

Possession is a phenomenon that intrigues and terrifies in equal measure. The whole idea of being taking over by an alien intelligence brings terror with it. But let us find a better way to understand this state. Possession indicates an alteration of consciousness; you are no longer yourself completely. There is indeed an intrusion from somewhere else at work. This intrusion can be from yourself, as a call from your ancestors, by blood or spirit, which addresses certain failures in your psychological make up that are in need of alignment. This usually takes the form of pretending to be possessed, to *give a performance*. This is an exercise of one's own psyche or soul born from a spiritual vibration. Even if it is not spirit possession in a useful way for the community, it is a state which is important for the individual and their growth. For the competent Tata or Yaya this should serve as a means for diagnosing the spiritual health of the person in question. These forms of possession are of a psychological nature, it is the soul that works on the person trying to tell them something with the aid of spirit. Such forms of possession are always blocked by true spiritual aspiration. If the Tata is honest in his vision the pathology presented can lead to great change and transformation. Those possessions that are born from our selves and not carrying the flame of spirit are important, but it is equally important to be honest about what we are dealing with. A public display of psychopathology is different from the prophetic message of spirit, but equally important for the growth of the person in question. Common perceptions are that a possession by the dead, by ancestors, takes on different qualities, it is usually not as flamboyant as the *possession of soul*, rather the medium tends to move, if moving at all, in stiff and rigid ways and the words and messages are presented with greater simplicity and often with still greater depth conveyed by their very simplicity. When *mpungo* comes it is a session of true miracles, because here we are introduced to a pure force of nature that knows human life and cosmic law equally. At times the presence of mpungo in a person gives rise to profound messages and yet others silence, but in these cases nature brings omens to be interpreted. Yet another mode is the change of sight.

At times the veil between the worlds is seen to fall and you see what is there, this sight can take form in the *mpaka vititi* or in the medium, but it often takes the form of inspiration. I personally consider being under the inspiration to be the most perfect form of possession because you do *see*, you really see what is around the person. Some people are gifted with the ability of sight and as such the interpretations are a gift gained by practice and the level of wisdom the soul manages to accumulate. It is here the Tata and Yaya falls from grace or are raised thereof.

Personally I believe there is less uniformity around the issue of spirit possession and I believe that when ancestor possession happens this naturally calls on mpungo. Here we have a great variety, from violent forms to barely noticeable breaths of wind announcing possession. The spirit meets with the medium and the spirit and medium in combination give a particular impression to a specific spirit denizen.

When it comes to the nkisi matters are slightly more complicated. The nkisi or nganga is your creation as a Tata. When this particular nkisi takes possession, you are taken by a composite of the dead (familiar or not), the mpungo that gives its orientation and also the extension of Nzambi within you, your soul's response to the divine. When the Tata enters into possession with his *nfumbe* (animated bones) he is colored by the world he created for the nfumbe and also his connection with Nzambi. The nkisi can therefore be many things – a prophetic vehicle, an exercise of complexes and the grace of Nzambi upon the world – and this is all in the hands of the Tata.

Possession can be felt like a power sitting on your shoulders that demands entry or it can hit suddenly like a whirlwind or lightning. It can come soft and mild, like a dream on the wings of night. After experiencing possession in many different contexts I would dare say that it is the state of dream that connects all these forms of possession together. This is because it is in the oneiric realm that the veil between the worlds is gone and here we can travel and manifest along the same forked road.

When a spirit or an ancestor arrives and wants to use your material body it will often identify itself in sympathy with the state of mind and soul you are in, it is crucial to understand that you make the bridge and provide the welcome. I believe that this is the most common form of possession, where the spirit is using the faculties of the medium to interact with the world. If this state is maintained and spirit is allowed to flow one can experience a general increase in presence until your own dismissal from your body which allows room for peaks or a steady presence to manifest. Here the spirit can break through and speak its native language and perform wondrous feats and miracles. Unfortunately many people have a resistance towards this complete surrender motivated by the belief of alien intrusion and fear of not being able to return to the human state of mind.

Some people prefer what in Cuba is called *two headed possession*, some will say it is bad, and others good. I am of the opinion that it is generally a good state, but difficult to maintain for a long time. It means that you and spirit occupy the same space and materiality at the same time. This places demands on the spiritual stature of the medium because two headed possession provides an avenue for acting out our own nature, and not that of the spirits. At times the medium can walk back and forth from advice and messages clearly of a nature not inspired by spirit to give astonishing prophetic advice and perform miracles. At times this form of possession is seen as less ideal but for me this is the ideal state of possession, given that you are of a good stature. After all, two headed possession provides a unique perspective upon the world mediated by your maturity as a human being – and herein lays its fallacy. If you are immature, this immaturity will seep out when the oracle is spoken because the soul wants to be known, mature or not. In a way, the medium is the battery of transition and herein lays its strengths and limitations.

To receive spirit demands openness and also control. The more one is subject to the whims and fancies of the spirit, the more intrusive it feels, and the more it speaks of the immaturity of the medium. Some Paleros refers to these people to have become *the dog of the prenda*, defining an inversion of the original agreement between the Ngangulero and the Nganga. The use of the word *dog* is frequent, and can be a reference to the Palero and the prenda, a remnant from slavery when *dog* was a unifying term both for Africans and Muslims used by the explorers.

The favored way of training ones mediumship in Palo Mayombe is in the Misa Espiritual, the Spiritual Mass. It is quite common that a Misa is performed prior to *rayamento* (initiation) so the spirit guides and ancestry of the aspirant is made known. A suggestion for this ceremony is presented in the appendix of this book.

THE FIRMAS

The *firmas* of Palo Mayombe are the spirit signatures. In the firmas we can see the essence of the nkisi and also what rama the signature derives from. For instance the firmas of Kimbiza tend to be all made within the Nzo Nzambi, the Church, while the ndoki ramas, like Changani are rougher and yet again the Brillumba seems to present a more elaborate cosmological presentation of the signature. The basic format of firmas consists of arrows, crosses and circles. The arrows represent directions, the circles possibilities, what is not yet manifest, the negative, and the crosses the positive presence of Nzambi. In this the world of Nzambi is described in its richness of possibilities. It does not really matter what symbols the different ramas apply, the basic ideas are still inscribed in ntoto and from this the firmas take life.

The firmas of Palo Mayombe are as important as the veves are in Vodou. Like the veves they are cosmograms revealing the essential nature of a given power. When the Ngangulero draws the firma and mutters the words of power the cosmogram becomes its representation. The firma when activated is like a prayer and a calling at the same time, it claims the attention of whom the signature belongs to.

When the African's arrived in Cuba they also entered into contact with the indigenous people there, the Taino. The Taino venerated a god, Yucahú that they considered an ancestral deity living in the mountains. This deity/ancestor had a brother, Huracan, who manifested in storms. Yucahú was a guard against storms and a provider of peace and fertility of the land through his wife, Attabeira, often conceived of as a giant turtle. For the Taino all things were *Cemi*, a word used to denote the common spiritual meeting point between a spirit and god and its material representation in the shape of vessels and signs. Human bones were important, as the bones were the ancestral memory and were treated accordingly. The vessels and the concepts would resonate well with the Africans, but in addition the Taino also used petroglyphs and markings in sand and wood to symbolize the presence of the Cemi. It seems that everything in existence was accompanied by a symbolic form that made the power manifest. It has been suggested that the Taino originally emigrated from the upper parts of present day Brazil, which might explain why we find similar beliefs and practices amongst Indian populations in the north-east of Brazil. It also provides an avenue of explanation for the presence of *pontos riscados* (marked points) in Umbanda and Kimbanda. It can also be noted that a need for symbolic representation increased with slavery as the slaves were often without their sacred spirit pots and vessels. No matter how we seek to explain this, the presence of firma/veve/pontos riscados is something clearly shared between Kongo inspired practitioners and Indians.

For the Africans this was merely a logical extension of representing the divine. The meeting with the Taino might have inspired the importance of firmas in Palo Mayombe as much as the Vodoun veve in Hispania. The firmas are essential; they serve as the password for the prenda to work and having the firma of your prenda you can bring its manifestation to whatever place the firma is drawn. All prendas have their own personal firma, which is the *tratado* or contract between the prenda and the Ngangulero.

THE VIBRANT BONEYARD

The Yowa is used in a most intriguing way in the rama of Palo Monte Briyumba Malongo. Here we find the *minkisi Angoro* and *Angoromea*. The basic firma is simple, it is a world separated by a cross that marks four fields. These fields are marked with two crosses in the upper half and two circles in the lower half. They are syncretised with the *Ibeji* or sacred twins in Santeria, but Angoro and Angoromea has little to do with the perception of twins in Santeria as they represent a far more traditional and true reflection upon the mystery of twins. Angoro and

Angoromea are said to be *chichirikús* that were stillborn and thus represented by a doll with a skeleton face. Angoro is said to have drowned in poisoned waters and thus the placenta is particularly sacred for him. He is said to be given life by Nzasi, the thunder. Angoromea is said to be female, similar in vibe to the Arará spirit Anabí. She is said to have been strangled by her umbilical cord and thus this cord as the hangman's noose is particularly sacred to her. She is said to be given life by Kalunga or rather Baluande. This twin mystery is in need of a further stellar counterpart to truly come to life. So, the Nzamba and red and white mpungo that takes its powers from the Sun is what animates Angoro and turn him into the Sun of death walking the earth. In the same manner, Ntala and blue and white mpungo who takes her powers from the moon animates Angoromea and turns her into the deadly moon walking the earth.

This mystery is descriptive of the sacred technology applied in Palo Mayombe. Bones are given life, both by the rituals of exhumation, the powers of earth — but also the influence of the stars — thus presenting a mystery veiled in nocturnal elegance.

The twin mystery in Palo Mayombe also provides an interesting connection to Gurunfinda, the Lord of Greenwood and his Yoruba counterpart Osanyin, whom in Cuba seems to have fused with him quite completely. It is namely with Osanyin/Gurunfinda the secrets of twins rests — and nowhere else. Gurunfinda is indispensable in Palo Mayombe; he is the animating power of nature. The life of our body is possible because of him. He possesses the secrets of earth and the leaves, the waters and the trees. When we pass away from this world our animated matter returns to nature, the field of his expertise. He is as important for Palo Mayombe to work as are the bones provided by Cubayende, the Boneherd himself. It is here Palo Mayombe unfolds, in the cemetery in the midst of the wild woods. This harmonious relationship is subject to several other impulses, everything carrying the starlight in the creation of Nzambi. Let us delve into this mystery that makes the world at night and day vibrant with power and creativity.

THE RETINUE OF NZAMBI

Nzambi is the also known as Nsambi, Sambia, Nsambiampungo, Pungun Sambia, Sambia Liri, Sambia Surukuru and Sambi Bilongo. It represents the distant and creative principle – and also the first ancestor.

Palo Mayombe holds two matters immaculately sacred: death and the wilderness. Death is the gate of certainty we must all pass through and it is the nfumbe, the bones themselves that represent nkuyu/ndoki/nkulu/bakulu – ancestry in all its possible reflections as it veils itself in the multicolored shrouds of death. Nfumbe finds its negative reflex in *nfuri*, the restless dead. The other matter is *nfinda*, the wilderness. Here in Nfinda we find the trees from whence the sticks (*palos*), leaves and branches so vital for Palo Mayombe are taken. The trees are ancestors – and they are divine, this is the traditional Kongo view of trees. They serve as ladders for divine presence upon earth and ancestors tend to linger around in the windy treetops with Nkuyu. The sticks are nkisi in the sense of *medicine*. Several sticks or medicines are *minkisi* and when prepared for use they are called *bankisi*. Still, nkisi, like the word kimbiza, means both medicine and nature in the sense of being wild and alive. Nkisi originated in Nzambi and it is said that the animating power of all nkisi when it came to earth took the shape of Funza, who was to be the ancestor of all men. Funza was given the task of endowing all things in nature with a particular power or medicine. We might say that nkisi became minkisi and generated bankisi through Funza's mission. Nkisi designates lifeforce or the power of creative being. Everything that is from Nzambi is potentially nkisi. Both man and nkisi are extensions of Nzambi. The difference might be that man is Nzambi's mirror through Funza while nkisi is the medicine of nature and cosmos, thus it makes up the world of possibilities for man. It is a particular gathering of nkisi, or powers that makes up the palero's spirit pot, the nganga, This word refers both to the pot itself as well as the one who owns the pot. By working nkisi you become nkisi. The nganga is composed from the spirit of a deceased one, represented by its bones, earth from various locations, minerals, animals, magical powders and the palos or sticks that are essential for giving life to the nkisi that is to live within the nganga. The nkisi/nganga communicates through dreams, possession, inspiration, and *shamalongos* (four disks made from coconut shell or large cowry shells used for divination. The nganga is also equipped with a *mpaka vititi*, also called *vititi mensú* – a horn filled with secrets of the nganga, complete with a mirror or glass that serves as the divinatory vinculum. The mpaka is the window out on the world for the nkisi.

Between the forces of nature (kimbiza/nkisi) and Nzambi we find *mpungo,* or *kimpungulu* in plural. The mpungo is the force behind the natural manifestations and powers. They can be equated with stars and planets and their attending spirits and intelligences. The most feared mpungo in Palo Mayombe today is perhaps Lukankazi/Kadiempemba, originally a sky god that in the process of conversion became syncretised with the Devil. Lunkankazi can be defined as the circle of fire that limits Nzambi's expression. He is not a diabolic force as such, but the limit of possibilities, the circumference that restricts movement. Then we have Cubayende/Tata Nfumbe who is the owner of death and disease, Lord Death if you will. He is assisted by Centella Ndoki/Mariwanga who is the graveyard itself and Cubayende the psychopomp who mediates between the dead and the living in the garden of Centella. Next in importance we find Gurunfinda, owner of the wild forests followed by Nkuyu/Lucero, a spirit of the wind that brings the parade of ancestors after him in the form of fireflies and stars. The ocean is called Baluande and Kalunga, and the river is known as Mama Chola Wengue. The mountain and its secrets are known as Tiembla Tierra/Mama Kengue and the hunters take the form of Zarabanda, the blacksmith and Watariamba/Vence Bataya master of the arrow and justice. Finally we find Nzasi who is the thunder and lightning. These are the most well known kimpungulu, but there are others, like Nganga Kissi/Kimbabula who is the mpungo of divination and Cuye Luamba, Lord of sorcery and knowledge and a host of other lesser known mpungos.

The nkisi is a natural power always existent but one that can also be manipulated into something else – something other, but still sacred. When the spirit pot, the nganga is assembled, it is often referred to as nkisi – the nkisi represented by the nganga is a composite of ancestry, mpungo and natural nkisi. What we gather in the pot resonates with the mpungo and not only gives life but also allows a cycle of expression to unfold. The nkisi that is created in the nganga is usually generated on the basis of a certain mpungo, who gives the nkisi its quality. It is the law of harmonies and sympathies which rules the creative mind that sets out to assemble the nganga. By gathering items that are in harmony with a higher principle (mpungo) the nganga turns into a body sparking with life which is given direction by the nfumbe and the pact that occurs between the Nganguelero (he who holds the nganga) and the nganga. The Nganguelero and the nganga become one. This means that minkisi is everywhere and man has a relationship to these ancestral forces. This ancestry can then be reclaimed and brought together again into a living unit that serves as man's medicine and companion. It is from this reuniting of the qualities of mpungo as manifested in numerous nkisi that brings to life a unique nkisi whose mystery lives on in the name it will be given when the pact is made between the spirit in the pot and him or her who is to hold it.

Palo Mayombe replicates the anguish related to death, violence and transformation in the transatlantic crossing but also in both Cuba and the singular span of a human life. It is a cult which speaks of acceptance, of the core and of being truthful in undergoing the challenge of transformation and change. We can say that Palo Monte and Mayombe originated in Cuba roughly in the 17th century, Lucumi originated in the 18th century and Santeria in the 20th century. Spiritism entered in the 19th century. Palo Mayombe was subject to all these influences but adopted little. The most significant adoption was perhaps Spiritism, as we find expressed in the Misa Espiritual, but this was in many ways a return to its roots, even though it is commonly referred to as Palo Cruzado. The spiritual misa has its basis in the Kongo kingdom, and the gentler ways of interacting with spirits that was also transported to Brazil and was developed into the established religion known as Umbanda. The prime emissaries of Umbanda were the Preto Velhos and Caboclos, the *old blacks* and *Indians* – in other words ancestry, and the new land spoke as one in Umbanda – as it did in the Misa Espiritual. As I see it, the Misa Espiritual represented a sort of compromise. It was important to maintain one's roots and culture, but over time the land defines its inhabitants and for each successive generation the perceptions of mystery will be shaped in conformity with the land. As such *espiritsmo de cordón* or the Misa Espiritual perhaps reflect in the deepest sense the common reference for contemporary Cuban spirituality by calling attention to the land itself. The land is what brings back the departed and renews them in the skin of the new land. In this Misa differences were bridged and autonomy defined in conformity with the spirits of the land, the multiple ancestries and the Taino. In spite of the difficulties presented in homogeneity of culture and spirituality due to the massive diversity of influences, Palo Mayombe managed to maintain a theology that set itself apart from the Yoruba inspired faiths that took shape. This was most likely caused by the last wave of the slave trade that blossomed into freedom with the Kongo legacy still fresh in its mind. Cuba had two big migrations of Bantu speaking people, one from 1596 until 1640 and then the last wave from 1831 to 1867. The latter migration was predominantly from the Cross river state of Carabali and Mayombe in the north-west of Kongo. And it is reasonable to believe it was the melée of cultures from this district that ended up shaping Palo Mayombe into what it is today.

The complexity of the cardinal concepts of Palo Mayombe, need to be addressed even more deeply, as they form the vertebrae of Palo Mayombe. Through these we can understand the practical and metaphysical composition of the spirit pot, the nganga:

Nfumbi are the physical bones, and in particular the cranium. The bones are believed to carry the awareness of the person from their entire life. The memories of the human condition are imprinted on the bones. This is why the skull is so treasured, it is the seat of consciousness. The various body parts continue to have a relationship with the world of the living when they are re-animated in the nganga. The foot is for movement, the hands for doing, the spine and sternum for support and so forth. Each bone possesses an awareness that can be used, or in some cases overridden. For instance, in Kimbiza orders that work in a highly spiritual way the use of bones is limited and when used they are employed in the form of a powder. The bone powder is used to quicken the awareness of mpungo upon earth. This can be done by simply assembling the *Igba Orisa* (the spirit pot of an Orisa) and quickening this with a selection of earth, herbs and bone powder. We might say that this is a technique where mpungo turns into nkisi. This process is quite different to Mayombe where nfumbe turns into nkisi, where the bones are worked as the central focus of the nkisi.

Ndoki, carries the shades and shadows of the person, it is the realm of impulses and bad memories. Consequently, some isolate the ndoki aspects in a separate vessel within the nganga. Some call this *chichereku* and understand it to be the most essential and true essence of the nfumbe/nfuri. Others say that the ndoki represents the malign ancestors or spirits. Yet others see the ndoki as the shadow side of the nganga. Ndoki is all of this and more as the term is actually more neutral in Bantu language, where it can be used as a reference to power in general. Ndoki is often a power that touches upon the supernatural and often the supernatural powers of the night, this being a manifestation of one's dreams, or an ability to effectuate supernatural harm. Nfumbe and ndoki forms the human psyche, the day and the night of our soul.

Mpungo is a superior consciousness, a quality of Nzambi. The power of a tree and the planets are mpungos, but the physical representation is nkisi. Everything that *is* has the color of Nzambi as expressed through mpungo – which is why a given nganga is often referred to by names of mpungos coupled with a specific name, such as Zarabanda Rompe Monte, Zarabanda being the mpungo of iron, Rompe Monte being the name of the nganga. Together they make up a unique nkisi. As such mpungo refers to something superior to simply the material. It is the intelligence and non-corporeal spirit that animates every material object and thing with life. It is the same animating power the Tata is using when a new nganga is given life and it is this animating principle that is remembered by naming a prenda a Zarabanda or a Nzazi or after any other mpungo. The mpungo represents a quality and this quality is replicated in all of nature and gives a cosmic quality to the nkisi, thus a nganga is named in respect of this quality.

A correctly made nganga nkisi will behave like a compass rose, constantly moving and revolving around its axis in a constant recreation of its possibilities in meeting with the *minkuyo* that rides upon the winds from all the corners of the world. It is these four factors that form the crossroad or *nzila* of the mystery of the spirit pot, the nganga. The nkisi assembled will use chamalaongos, mpaka vititi and the vinculum held by the Ngangulero for possession in order to make itself known through conversations and *bilongos* (works).

The nganga nkisi is a unique world, a microcosm that through its contents resonates with all of nature. The centre and the soul of this new world are made aware through the nfumbi and the ability of the nganga to resonate with mpungo. To this are added the *macutos* (charms/amulets), the *bilongos* (workings) the *mpolos* (powders), *firmas*, *mbele* (blade), the powers of the cat, the dog, the rooster, the vulture and the eagle. By conjuration and blood, the nkisi comes together as a lycanthropic creation that travels within earth as well as on the winds, the manifested powers of the primordial sorcerer stored within the original witch's cauldron, now named and conscious.

The nkisi nganga actually becomes a part of the family. Upon initiation it is the nganga of the Tata that begets children and grandchildren and not the Tata himself. It is to the nkisi that respect and reverence are directed. The intrinsic nature of the nganga reveals a natural tendency towards evolution and thus variations of a highly personal nature should take form on the Kalunga of the Ngangulero. This because what was dead is now alive – but reassembled in a unique way that brings something back from beyond the veil that separates the world of the dead and the living and fuses it with this world and the Ngangulero in the form of the nganga, the body that holds it's consciousness.

The oldest prenda in Cuba is said to date back to the late 17th/early 18th century, and is called Vititi Congo Saca Empeño in Guanabacoa. It is fairly common to trace ones ancestry back to this original prenda. For Palo Mayombe this prenda is the first ancestor of the cult. There are rumors of a nganga even older dating to around 1580 that gave birth to the father prenda of Vititi Congo Saca Empeño.

THE LINEAGES OF PALO MAYOMBE

There are many lineages or ramas of Palo Mayombe and significant for the multitude of ramas is the work of Siete Brillumba Congo. This rama was born when seven Brillumba Tatas combined their ngangas to create a *Nsasi Ndoki*. This Brillumba has grown through the years and it appears to me that it has contributed to less rigidity towards the nature of ones rama, as the ramas in general became more fused and greater interaction was accomplished both through Brillumba Palo and also through Kimbiza. It might be more proper to refer to the ramas as expressing themselves within *Reglas* or Laws, of which we have three main *Reglas de Palo*, Brillumba, Mayombe and Kimbiza. There are several ramas or lineages of palo, such as Changani, Chamalongo, Kimbisa, Briyumba Palo Monte, Corta Lima; and most of them curiously draw their lineage somehow back to Andres Petit and his Kimbisa order. In spite of many ramas we can separate them into three different reglas, or rules.

We can make a distinction between these three rules in terms of their perception of the nganga and how to work the nfumbe. Mayombe is a continuation of a particular cult from the hills of Mayombe in the areas of Cabinda and Calabari in Kongo that was brought to Pinar del Rio in Cuba. Mayombe focuses on the mystery of the *nfuri of the mountains* and its technology is the origin of what today is referred to as prenda ndoki. A prenda ndoki will use as its prime possession the *kiyumba* (skull) of a dead palero in his spiritual ancestry. Then we have Kimbiza which arrived in Cuba already subject to Christian syncretism, with a heavy focus on mpungo and saints. This friendliness towards syncretism resulted in Kimbiza Palo which was reformed by Andres Petit and became assimilated with Orisa and even Ifá. This is evident in Petit's Kimbiza today, which advocates the possession of as many ngangas as possible and a more elaborate hierarchy that adopted technology and rituals from Lucumi and Santeria, like the role of the Oriaté in Santeria being turned into the office of Tatandi in Kimbiza. In Santeria you need an Oriate who possesses the knife (i.e. the right to perform lifeforce offerings) present to effectuate the rituals and make them valid. In the same manner, the Tatandi of Kimbiza by receiving the *mbele*, the equivalent to receiving the knife in Ocha, is needed to effectuate initiations and found a munanso. The assimilation with Lucumi resulted in the Kimbiza prendas being quite similar to the Igba Orisas through the focus on mpungo. The focus is less on the nfumbe than it is on the mpungo. In Kimbiza the mpungo is the important nucleus. Brillumba, on the other hand, is the opposite; the nfumbe is endowed with mpungo and nkisi qualities and becomes the centre of the nganga and is given a spiritual path. Kimbisa creates a harmonious world, Brillumba creates a world for the nfumbe and Mayombe resurrects the nfuri/nfumbe void of syncretism.

This means that we have essentially three reglas of Palo Mayombe with a wide array of offshoots and interactions, meetings and *tratados* or agreements between the ramas. These are:

> *La Regla Mayombe*
> *La Regla Brillumba/Vriyumba*
> *La Regla Kimbisa*

As we have mentioned, Mayombe gained its name from a specific geographical location, namely Mayombe. Although Natalia Bolivar has suggested, in conformity with Lydia Cabrera's suggestion, that it means *superior/chief* – in the sense of someone who is dominating the cult, nature and the nfumbe – replicating the status of the manikongo. Most likely this interpretation is a Cuban one, and the Mayombero is understood on the basis of its origin in contemporary Cuba. Mayombe is also considered to be Palo void of saints and thus belongs to the more dangerous or ndoki stratas of the cult. Brillumba, also known as Vriyumba, defines the nature of the cult and not a specific place. The word Vriyumba is of kikongo origin and is composed of *yúmba* which signifies the spirit of a departed one and *vili*, which both denotes a native of Angola but also *works*. Vriyumba thus means *to work the spirit of death*. Closely related is the work *kiyumba*, meaning skull, but as we see from the word *yúmba* it is specifically an animated skull which it refers to. The prepared skull was amongst the bakongos called *nyúmbila*, and the gathering of offensive and protective herbs conjoined with life-giving herbs and bilongos would reveal an agreement with the inner secrets of the Vriyumba mysteries.

There is one other term that surfaces from time to time, this is the kikongo *Nkita* – and there are some ramas that use this term in reference to its lineage. Nkita was a name given to diviners and healers societies in Kongo, more specifically the Angolan part. The word defines the spirit of the deceased, but in particular one who exerts its terrestrial influence by haunting wells, watery ravines and creeks. Vermin issuing from polluted water and fertile organisms are its messengers which represents its day side and night side. The word nkita was also used as an alias for mpungo, often understood on the basis of it taking serpentine form. Overall these spirits maintain an association with water and death, as the nfumbe holds with the Kalunga, the abysmal waters, the deep liquid space of ancestral wisdom. It does seem that it might represent a specific class of departed ones that lived on in the mysteries of Simbi in Haitian Vodou – a Kongo mystery, the *kisimbi*.

It is widely accepted that the Kimbisa order was founded by a Cuban Criollo of Haitian ancestry named Andrés Facundo Cristo de Dolores Petit (1830–1878). Andrés Petit, or Andrés Quimbisa (as both he and his successor were called) is a figure of mythic proportions in Afro-Cuban religion. He provokes a great diversity of opinion, but regardless of one's view, it is not possible to avoid the legacy of Andres Petit. He is credited with instigating a major syncretism of various elements of religious and spiritual practice found in Cuba into a new and uniquely Cuban religion, known as La Regla Kimbisa del Santo Cristo del Buen Viaje. Petit's order combined elements from Abakuá, Espiritismo, Masonry, Ocha, and Christianity but with a strong and omnipresent Congo foundation. Petit's Kimbisa order focused on religious devotion as much as mystical practices and bilongos. It is however important to point out that some Paleros referred to themselves as Kimbiseiros prior to Petit's founding of his Kimbisa order. It seems likely that Petit developed his Kimbisa Order around a kernel of a more arcane Kimbisa rama probably related to the Abakuá secret society. Petit is likewise credited with contributing to the survival of the Abakuá society by admitting politically well-connected white people and creoles. Since Abakuá used to be a society restricted to blacks, Petit's wider recruitment was met with resistance and he was for some time seen as a traitor who sold the Abakuá secrets for personal gain. His supporters considered this a politically correct move and also point out that the initiations Petit conferred were done solely at the cost of materials involved, hence the allegation of personal profit were proved false. The rest of his life and actions, to the extent it can be verified, gives testimony to an altruistic and serious spiritual individual of an ecumenical and well intentioned disposition.

Today, several legitimate lineages of his Kimbisa order survive worldwide. Petit's strict focus on what is good and the Christian elements has however been 'crossed' over the years, testifying to the dynamic nature within Palo Mayombe. The diversity amongst Kimbiseiros might also testify that the Kimbisa order of Petit and the rama he developed it from continued in a slightly different form although in harmony with the original spiritual and metaphysical ideas.

All prendas carry the name of their rama. As mentioned, the prenda is given the name of a mpungo, then the nkisi is given a name, sometimes this is called baptism, and then the rama is added as a family or last name. For example, a prenda made with the vibration of Zarabanda and given the name Rompe Monte will have its complete name by adding the name of the rama, which identifies it as a particular member of a specific family. In this case it could be Zarabanda Rompe Monte Brillumba Kimbisa. This name speaks of the presence of Zarabanda in a given quality or road, as *the power of iron who breaks mountains by the powers of Brillumba and Kimbisa.*

The reglas of Palo Monte Mayombe follow the same degree structure, and some orders have further secret degrees linked to particularly hot mysteries. This is not much different from affiliations with secret societies in Haitian Vodou, these societies often being of the Kongo nations, such as bizango and sanpwel. The degrees are as follows:

First we have the *Ngueyo* also known as *Pino Nuevo*, or new branch, and *Muchacho de Prenda*. In this stage the one who is to be admitted to the rama is considered to be the new branch on the ramas tree. The

Ngueyo is scratched (*rayado*) over the nganga of his Tata or Yaya and a pact is made with the nganga of the Ngueyo's Tata. This step involves defining the particular path the Ngueyo has in Palo Mayombe and what mpungo he or she resonates with. He or she will then receive training in accordance with the oracles.

The second step is *Tata Nkisi* and is more of a step achieved by ones work. When a certain mastery of the cult is obtained, especially in relation to the Nfinda (wilderness) and bilongos (magical works) through alignment with mpungo this degree is ceremonially conferred upon the Ngueyo. The Tata or Yaya Nkisi does not possess the priced prenda which is the third step on the ladder of growth.

A *Tata Nganga*, also called Padre/Madre Nganga or Ngangulero is the Tata or Yaya who is in possession of their own prenda. At this stage a pact is made with ones own prenda and this completes the Palero. In most reglas, the Ngangulero is considered to be competent enough to form a munanso, a house of Palo and to induct Nguyos into his or her munanso.

There are also other titles given, such as *Tata Ndibilongo*, which etymologically denotes someone with a deep knowledge of bilongos and the technologies of magical works, but is commonly a reference to a Ngangulero who has godchildren. Then there is the title *Tata Luwongo*, which is only applicable when a munanso has grown into a second generation of Paleros, where the Ngangulero receiving this title is considered *avuelo de prenda*, or godfather of foundation – the prenda who founded the munanso.

II NGANGA NKISI

RESURRECTIONEM MORTUORUM

The roots of language are irrational and of a magical nature.*

The resurrection of the dead, to reanimate corpses and to bring life to forms and images is not something exclusive to Palo Mayombe. It is more the particular modus operandi and purpose that deviates from the necromantic arts in Antiquity which informed Western ideas of necromancy.

Necromancy is more than just calling forth the departed ones; it is part of a greater labyrinth. Necromancy can be understood to make up part of the larger realm of Theurgy. I would suggest that the equivalent of the palero is found in the nigromancer. The nigromancer was a person who was expert in spirit trafficking. He was essentially the type of practitioner that worked on both poles of the axis of the world. The necromancer and nigromancer are commonly understood to be identical to one another, but it would suffice to point out that *necro*, to work with shells and cadavers, is different from *niger*, black, with a direct reference to works with nocturnal spirits. I believe this goes deeper: *niger* would for the nigromancer be the revelation of Saturn at work. Saturn as earth, as putrefaction, poison, the Venus secret and King of the Golden Age would all comprise this idea of *niger*. For the nigromancer the interaction with the infernal and celestial are part of the greater focus on a spirit communion largely erected on Hyperborean premises. If this is a worthy description of the nigromancer, it is here we find a more truthful relationship with the *goes*, from whence we have the popular term *goêteia*, relentlessly associated with infernal spirits and demons. Goêteia describes more a set of practices, a techné for dealing with restless and violent spirits of all sorts that made life for the living turbulent. The goes were especially skilled in funeral rites and crossroad mysteries. At times the goes are separated from the magoi and

* Jorge Luis Borges.

their wonder-workings, but this might be rooted in a Nabatean distinction placing a greater focus on astrology and celestial image magic rather than the chthonic realms. What both the magoi and the goes had in common was what the Chaldean Julianas coined *theourgia*/theurgy in the 1st century CE. Theurgy is a neo-Platonic concept that reveals the need for understanding the sympathy between all forces divine, celestial and terrestrial and how they connect to man. It advocates an intelligent use of these celestial and terrestrial harmonies born from a deep understanding of the laws of nature.

The idea of reanimation is not a strange one in the history of mankind's magical practices. In the Norse *Ynglingasaga* we read the following:

> *They took Mime, therefore, and beheaded him, and sent his head to the Aesir. Odin took the head, smeared it with herbs so that it should not rot, and sang incantations over it. Thereby he gave it the power that it spoke to him, and discovered to him many secrets.*

A similar theme might be found in *Matthew* and *Mark* where we are told of the beheading of St. John the Baptist at the request of Herodias. *Mark* 6 in particular could be interesting to analyze in terms of the greater motive of the walking dead and resurrection. But this would be a lengthy exegesis, we shall be content here with simply referring to the end of the story where St. John's head is presented to Salome on a silver platter and she gives the head to her mother Herodias, an important figure in European Witchcraft.

Rabbi Löw made his golem in 16th century Prague. Dr. Frankenstein, as a scientific successor of Erictho, made his monster, testifying to the possibility of cadavers and the earth being struck with the life giving flash of divinity. Ghosts, revenants and vampires have been resurrected willingly and unwillingly for millennia. Angels and spirits have taken on physical shape by creating a simulacrum from the elements or entering a vacant object. In a way it is enough to look at nature and how plants are reanimated after death to find a demonstration of this sympathetic nigromantic mystery.

NECROMANCY AND GOD MAKING

The most famous account of god-making is found in the *Corpus Hermeticum* in Asclepius, chapters 23–4 and 37–8. Here we can read the following:

> *... in this way Mankind, always mindful of its nature and origin, persists in imitating the Divine to the point that, just as the Father and the Lord endows the gods with immortality, in order that they may resemble Him, so mankind fashions its gods in its own image.*

> *... of herbs, stones and spices containing occult divine power. And if you would know why they are diverted with frequent sacrifices, hymns, songs of praise and concord of sweet sounds that imitate heavens harmony, it is so that that celestial element which has been enticed into the image by repeated celestial rites may in happiness endure its long sojourn among human kind. That then is how Man makes gods.*

It is proper that these chapters are given to Asclepius, who was paid handsomely by Artemis to resurrect Hippolytus from the dead. An act Zeus deemed unnatural and thus he sent a bolt of lightning which struck Asclepius dead. The birth of Asclepius speaks of his connection with corpses as his mother, Coronis – a mortal – was killed by her lover/husband Apollo for an act of infidelity. However, in her womb rested Asclepius, whom Apollo snatched from the cadaver and gave to the Centaur Chiron to raise. Chiron taught him the arts of healing and herbs. It is also said that Athena gave him a specific gift, a potion made from the blood of Gorgons. This potion could both resurrect and bring death. Upon entering the world Asclepius served as a healer and doctor for humankind and it was because of his many good deeds that Zeus made him immortal and placed him in the constellation of the Ophiuchus (the serpent bearer) as a reference to his cunning concerning the medicinal use of serpents and vipers. A significant part of his healing was to place the afflicted in a dormitory with snakes and during the night a god or spirit would enter into their dreams and his priesthood would interpret the oracular message. Asclepius finds a resonance in the Pythagorean king Zalmoxis, a friend of Hades who knew immortality, something Plato related in *Charmides*. Zalmoxis is acredited with the power of charms, death and wisdom, making him a worthy image of Asclepius.

The presence of snakes and the use of honey and herbs in the process of reanimation seem to be a recurring theme no matter where in the world we turn. In addition the heads needed a set of written charms (*voces magicae*) that for the goes were written on a flax or bay leaf with either myrrh ink or the blood of a dead man and placed in its mouth. Honey, herbs and enchantments are what the serpent binds to make a head oracular.

The Greek sources that were instrumental in passing this heritage to Roman practitioners are the accounts of Lucan, Apuleius and Heliodorus. These three typify the Egyptian-Hellenic succession of magic that occured in Antiquity. Another thing these have in common is their focus on the wickedness of the witches of Thessaly. It might be the magical practices preserved in Thessaly that we find in the Greek Magical Papyri.

Lucan's Erictho came to be the icon of the malevolent witch in the Western world. She reanimates corpses by prayers, charms and invocations, herbs and hot blood. She first summons the ghost to appear and then directs it back to the body through its death-giving wound. In like manner, the witch Bessa uses the same elements but also applies fire and libations as part of the summoning.

Erictho calls on Hecate, Hades, Persephone, Earth and Night to enflame her work, both celestial and infernal. She works with a black sheep, honey and milk to produce a hot blood that can reanimate a corpse. It is from the stories of Erictho we find obscure ingredients thrown into the witches' cauldron, such as moonwater, dragon eyes, eagle stones, parts from the sea-monster *echenais*, foam from a dog with rabies and other impossible – or perhaps symbolic – ingredients. Ovid's Medea uses similar ingredients in her necromantic work, but also the guts of a werewolf, a crows head and the wings of a bat. Erictho is also mentioned in Dante's *Divine Comedy* where she is relegated to the innermost circle of hell, the punishment for those who resurrect the dead.

Pliny in his *Natural History* says that the ghost of Homer had been summoned by the herb *cynocephalia* (dog head) also known as Osiritis, said to be the herb that brought Osiris back to life. It is speculative, but since the name itself refers to werewolves, although in this context refers to a herb, we can only guess at Wolfsbane/Aconite being the candidate for the reanimating plant. They bring death – yet to what is already dead perhaps, like the Gorgon's blood, they bring life? If so we have here a most interesting connection between Homer and St. Christopher. Not only are they both travelers, but they also have shapeshifting in common. Homer was transformed by the hand of Circe into a wild hog and St. Christopher was in the middle Ages depicted in the Orthodox Eastern Churches as a *cynocephali* – a dogheaded saint. The Germanic bishop Speyer (967–1027) calls him the *canis from Canaan* and relates that he was saved by baptism from his unfortunate state.

Two other plants occur frequently, fennel and bay laurel. A fennel stalk is said to be what Prometheus used to steal the fire of the gods and it is also the stalk that was used by the brothers of The Horseman's Word in Britain to subdue and control both spirits and horses. Laurel with its associations of peace and victory is also a plant of the Sun, which in Mesopotamian and Greek lore was seen as the power of releasing ghosts and spirits at night – when absent. Cephalomancy, which is the name given to the use of oracular heads is testified as far back as Mesopotamia and manipulated by the *manzazu*. A Babylonian tablet speaks of Solar Shamash as *the skull of skulls*, and the one who is able to make skulls oracular. The Solar motive surfaces again with the head of Orpheus drifting ashore on the island of Lesbos and being taken care of by the muses. Orpheus had been torn into shreds by the Thracian maenads for having ceased worship of Dionysus in favor of his father Apollo. On the island of Lesbos it is said that the head *gave out oracles from a hollow in the earth* which seems quite similar to the oracle in the temple of Apollo at Delphi. Keeping in mind that Circe and Medea were respectively daughter and granddaughter of the Sun, it casts the principle of life-giving warmth and heat in a most peculiar light.

Other famous oracular heads include the one kept by Cleomenes I of Sparta who maintained the head of his friend Archonides in a jar of honey and conversed with it prior to any important task. We also learn of one Polycritus who died shortly after making his wife pregnant. The child was born a hermaphrodite and the dead father surged up from the halls of Hades and consumed the child leaving only the head. The head became oracular and uttered prophecies of doom. Yet another interesting case is the Roman general Publius who was consumed by a red wolf. The wolf consumed his body, but not the head which was preserved as it had become oracular. The presence of werewolves, the red wolf and the Sun, or perhaps its chosen absence, is quite intriguing and should be carefully noted.

In all cases of reanimation, herbs are important. Erictho uses not only herbs but also blood and magical items to reanimate the corpse. The cadaver is then beaten with a snake in order for it to gain life. Bessa on the other hand places the corpse between the grave and the fire and utilizes a poppet simulacrum of the corpse in her necromantic work whilst whispering her enchantments into the ear of the corpse. In similar ways the witch Zatchlas brings Thelyphron back to life by presenting herbs to his mouth and chest. In all of these cases the ghost was summoned and thus commanded into an existing body, something that Daniel Ogden suggests made blood sacrifice unnecessary. It seems that blood sacrifice or a lifeforce offering is necessary only when a corpse is artificially made, for instance when assembling the vital natural elements to animate a statue. In Apuleius' *Metamorphoses* we can read how Zatchlas resurrects into the flesh Thelyphron – and how Socrates receives life again by the hand of the Thessalian nigromancer Meroe. In a similar manner Aeson receives life again in Ovid's *Metamorphoses* and in Lucan's *Philopseudes* it is said that the Hyperborean sages know the art of resurrecting even decaying corpses – a power also attributed to the Chaldeans. This observation supports my own suggestion of nigromancy being ultimately a Hyperborean art.

In the Greek Magical Papyri we find several formulæ for reanimating a corpse. These rituals make admonitions to the spirit of the air to enter a specific body and rouse it by the power of God and in the name of

Thoth/Hermes – again a Hyperborean reference to the secrets resting in Adocynt, the City of Hermes. Hermes-Thoth is seen as the creator behind the oracular skulls. In the Greek Magical Papyri we find several spells and summarized they can be presented as follows:

> *Face east at sunset, invoke the Sun over the skull cup (skyphos) of a man who died violently.* {The skull cup might refer to the skull held upside down and thus being subject to receive libations and liquids}
>
> *Burn amara (sun beetle) mixed with frankincense.*
>
> *You will then take your ink made from the blood of a snake and blacksmith's soot to inscribe the proper voces magicae.* {i.e. charms and spells on the skull}
>
> *You will then repeat this with ink made from myrrh written on bay leaves, thirteen in number, and adorn the crown of the skull with them. It is said that doing this, Helios, the Sun, will then send the ghost of the skull at the hour of midnight* {or perhaps the thirteenth hour?} *to commune and give oracular answers to its maker.*

Similar procedures are also found using the skulls of animals and the elements are often the same: violent death, myrrh, flax, ivy and bay leaves.

A Byzantine spell suggests taking the head to the river and rinsing it for three days and three nights in the current. You will then wrap it in linen and take it to the crossroads where the crossroad-charms are written on its forehead. Daniel Ogden recounts a similar working from the *Codex Parisinnus Gr. 2419* where the names written are Bouak, Sariak and Lucifer. The skull is then placed on the skin of a black cat and taken to the crossroads at midnight. A circle is marked with a piece of dead man's rib and the head is left until cocks crow when the head is retrieved. The head turns oracular upon three days fasting, and works only at night. Another French Codex – *Bononiensis 3632/Delatte* – speaks of the use savory and the plant mercury (*mercurialis perennis* or Dog's mercury), a very toxic plant, to make a heavy ointment for the forehead, nape and the top of head of the skull which prior to its libation is inscribed with charms in a way that forms a cross. Five names in all should be inscribed, one on each night. On the fifth night the skull is taken to the crossroads and stays there until sunset. Upon getting the head one needs to dress in a clean robe, a cat skin belt and invoke the 'demons' with branches of laurel in the name of Jesus Christ.

It is obvious that the reanimation of corpses and cadavers was intimately linked with were-animals and perhaps vampires. Our sources Lucan and Apuleius speak of how dogs and wolves are always lurking close to specters and ghosts and ties them in with Hecate, grand symbol of the crossroads ignited by Helios himself, as the devotee. Herodotus speaks of the *Neuri* (sorceresses) who once a year transform into wolves. Virgil's Moeris could also turn himself into a wolf, and the wild hunt of Odin, the *einherjar*, were frequently said to dress in wolf skins, similar to the berserkers.

The practice of luring ghosts into statues was attested in Greece from the 4th century BCE. Likewise, the same techniques were used to make the ghosts enters jars and bowls of water and wine to give oracles. Some of this seeped into the nigromantic manual known as *The Testament of Solomon* which became the predecessor of all the goetic manuals. Here we find, particularly in the bottle spells, an interesting continuation of the necromantic practice with a further reference to the witch bottles.

These haunted statues could be chained or placed out in the wilderness depending on the nature of the cult surrounding its practice. Statues could carry the dead and gods and were the subject of veneration and offerings, much like the household cult of the *lares* in Roman homes. This would suggest that the idea of necromancy breaches the boundaries of communication with the dead and is in a broad sense the art of igniting life in inanimate matter. The first necromantic act occurred in *Genesis* when God breathed life into the muddy shell of Adam. Necro, although signifying corpse or shell, can be used in reference to a once living body that has suffered death, as much as a lifeless body, such as a statue, *mumia* or a talisman. Its reanimation was the result of herbs, honey and the involvement of the Sun, even if implied by its very absence.

DE ARCANA MORTIS

Necromancy can be understood as having its roots in ancestor veneration. All African cultures and all Mesopotamian, Babylonian, Greek
and Roman cultures had a notion of ancestry. The notion of ancestry
lives on today, but more as a social consideration where someone from
a family of ill-repute tends to suffer stigma from this and is treated
badly. In the past, ancestry was of greater importance for the whole
population and not something reserved only for kings, queens and aristocrats. A son or daughter was often judged by the accomplishments
of their parents and the reputation of their family. When the ecclesiastical demand of burying the deceased ones in cemeteries was set in
motion they also instigated the process of the dissolution of ancestral
awareness. Before this ecclesiastical demand the ancestors were buried
in their own land, and preferably inside the house. The living and the
dead continued to co-exist. This is wonderfully attested to in the works
of Claude Lecouteux speaking of the medieval mindset amongst the
Nordic people concerning death. He postulates that the ecclesiastical
usurpation of private faiths into a collective mystery contributed greatly to turning the corporeal revenant into a disembodied ghost. The
revenants were not errant spirits, but bound to hearth and land and by
all measure it seems that the sighting of once resurrected ancestors got
less and less frequent with fewer and fewer home burials. With the arrival of the cemetery a different mystery entered the world as ancestors
were gradually transformed into ghosts and increasingly draped in the
veils and colours of the demonic and forbidden. As such the cemetery
became the land of the crossroads for known and anonymous ancestors
and spirits of a nocturnal disposition.

The necromancer was engaged in rites forbidden since the time of
the Hebrew's wandering the desert. *Deuteronomy* condemns conjuration
and communion with the dead as an outlandish and heathen practice,
undertaken by the Canaanites. The reasons for this might be rooted
in their own lack of ancestral remains, leading to a lack of ritual loci,
or it might be condemnation rising from the idea that only God was
permitted to meddle with the natural order. During the Middle Ages,

Hades was transformed into Purgatory and, as such, an infernal forbidden region. At the same time the cult of death was maintained in the cult of the saints as a lawful way of communing with the dead. There are naturally many currents at play here and a complete picture would need to take into account the beliefs held on the sacred, transmigration, the nature of the soul, the nature of divination and oracles, the theological drift towards establishing ideas of Hell and Purgatory and also the relationship between Purgatory, the 'Fairy realm' and Hades. We should also include the Arabic influences on magical and theological thought since the 12th century. This must then all be mirrored by the development of necromancy as an oracular and divinatory art in Mesopotamia and in Antiquity through to its medieval association with the summoning of nefarious entities. Not only this, but the role of the Sun, whether as Shamash, Helios or Apollo walks through this mystery as a golden thread of light and fire.

With all these considerations taken into account we might define necromancy today as a form of spirit summoning that is Saturnine in nature. By this I mean that it is about conjuring the spirits of earth, be they ancestors or nocturnal spirits. It is about pacts and communion to establish helpful spiritual alliances. It is a work which involves working with 'the bones of the forest', roots, leaves and sticks and the spirits connected to putrefaction and material change. If we add fire, sulfur and mercury to this saturnine formula we arrive at a classification of necromancy that is touching upon the nigromantic arts and finds resonance with Kongo spirituality and Palo Mayombe. In the vocabulary of the Kongo, it could be about the relationship between *bakulu* (ancestor/spirit/ghost), *mvumbi* (cadaver) and *nkisi* (spirit) in relation to the idea of *ndoki* (power, usually with a nightside flavor).

Looking at the conception of the soul held amongst the Kongo this suggestion will become even more plausible, as the soul could wander in the forest of matter for years on end, influencing life side by side with the spirits. The proper name for an ancestral vessel amongst the Nganga Ngombo or diviner was *lukibi lwa bakulu* – vessel that guards the bones of the ancestor. This would be a succession of one's blood lineage in a divinatory vessel tapping into the collective memory of one specific family. We might say this gives a unique perspective upon matters in accord with one specific transmission of ancestral wisdom. The prenda in Palo Mayombe is rarely constructed upon the bones of one's blood ancestors and thus it is more properly a *nzo nkisi*, a spirit guarding my house. The nzo nkisi could be made founded on human bones and infused with an errant soul. The ensouled vessel would then be adopted as a part of the family and a spiritual lineage would either continue or be newly established.

Kongo cosmology holds that the soul, *nsala*, is a gift to men from Nzambi. The soul enables man to understand Nzambi and it is this understanding that fortifies man's ability to create. The creative power is manifested in the *kimbangu*, or mountain, which represents the *Ngolo*, the power behind every creative act. The nsala is the storehouse of ancestral memory called *luzcena* in kikongo and means simply *head* but in use refers to the activities of the mind. The nsala lives in the luzcena, the head as seat of the intellect and manifests in rational and logical thinking. The soul is a rational category, replicating the creative intellect of Nzambi.

The Yowa cosmogram is utilized to describe all and every cyclical phenomena and as such it also demonstrates the soul's journey from daybreak to daybreak. As the night falls on mundane life the nsala breaks free from its body and turns into a light. Phenomena of lights moving in the night are often seen as ancestors stirring until the daybreak of their next incarnation. We find the number nine occurring in relation to death. Many Kongolese believes the nsala should only stay a cycle of nine days, weeks, months or years without a body. Failing a union with matter it will at the end of its destined cycle be forced to merge with the body of a challenged person, that is one suffering from any abnormal state afflicting the brain, whether loss of faculties or psychological disorder. This is traditionally seen as a form of resistance towards manifesting one's journey.

The soul will then contribute to a form of cosmic restoration on a greater scale. The journey is important as it contributes to an evolution of ones heavenly and invisible principle that rests in the divine. It is as if the souls evolution is made possible by involution and living a life in matter. Terrestrial manifestation is seen as an opportunity to make the soul wiser, an opportunity to master and dominate the physical world. From this idea of the soul's constitution and purpose it is possible to explore philosophies more dense and mystical, as in the Kimbisa order and orders with a more existential approach, such as Changani and many Briyumbas, compared to the more prophetic and stoic stance held by some Mayomberos.

These perspectives assign the soul of the departed to become part of a greater fold of spirits manifesting in flashes of light and wandering lights in the night. We have the nocturnal focus, the solar presence and the whole saturnine array of workings that constitutes the rough framework for the nigromantic arts in the Creole sorcery we know as Palo Mayombe.

THE MYSTERY OF GOLGOTHA

When the Capuchin missionaries arrived on the shores of Kongo and spoke about Jesus Christ it was not difficult for the Kongolese to see nkisi. Crucifixes were within a short time being used as symbols for nkisi and crosses as symbols for the positive presence of Nzambi. The idea of prophecy was present in the many healers and diviners societies, and the idea of being sons and daughters of God was also present. The reanimation of cadavers was nothing new for them either, so when the story of the most famous of the returning dead, Jesus Christ, was presented as a hope for the future it clearly made sense. Seeing the mystery of Jesus' death in relation to the transubstantiation of the bread and the wine, the turning of lifeless substances into nkisi was another familiar elaboration to the Kongolese. If we undress the Christian mysteries from their dogmas, laws and hierarchies a quite magnificent deeper mystery appears.

Jesus Christ when he was about to be crucified was brought to Golgotha, which means *the place of the skull*. This might carry references to the secret spoken of in the Babylonian tablet of Shamash, where the Sun is seen as the skull of skulls. Here, at the mountain, also an important symbol of divine presence in the world for the Kongo, Jesus was hung upon the Yowa cosmogram where his soul undertook a journey free from the body before it manifested in a cadaver and came to life. This has significant resonance with the necromantic Arcanum.

If we turn towards Europe, the Christian mystery as presented by the Catholic Church met little resistance amongst pagans in terms of the cult of saints and the Eucharist. In fact it seems that the idea of the old religion was a reference to the Catholic Church which was losing ground to the Anglican and Lutheran movements, as born out in Emma Wilby's research . There is something quite profound in the mystery of the crucifixion at the place of the skull and its Eucharistic reflex speaks loudly about the necromantic possibilities this presents. The problem seemed not to be so much if it was possible to commune with the dead and spirits of the night, but rather the legality of such practices according to ecclesiastical law and doctrine.

When the Church made use of their minor ordinations one of them was the degree of the exorcist. In reference to the Book of Consecrations Richard Kieckhefer says that the text *explicitly speaks of the necromancer as an exorcist*. This might be verified in the use of the red book of exorcisms as the tool of the 'ex-pellar', or Cornish pellar, in their craft. A use that was also replicated in Scandinavia and Iceland, then in the hands of priests and bishops expelling bad spirits, just as Jesus Christ and his followers were charged with doing. To expel or exorcise was an office completely related to the arts of the necromancer and the goes as specialists in dealing with troublesome spirits. As the minor ordinations faded away from the ecclesiastical canon their nature and office was maintained in what we refer to today as the Solomonic Tradition.

THE FUNDAMENTO & ITS SECRETS

The mpungo represents the non-corporeal extension of Nzambi in the world. Mpungo is the spirit that ignites qualities in the world of manifestation. It is here we find the idea of the nkisi, which is the manifestation of a power caught in a specific time and moment, ruled by specific variables that generate its unique nature. Nkisi can therefore be taken to represent the plethora of spiritual potencies created and made manifest by a variety of mpungos and powers in the world. In Palo Mayombe this distinction is not subject to rigor, as often the differences are intuitively understood. For instance, Nsasi – the power of the thunder and lightning – is both mpungo and also the name of an nkisi. Nsasi as cosmic potential is mpungo, but manifest in the form of the spirit vessel it is nkisi. When Nsasi is manifest it gains a unique name. This can for instance be *Nsasi Malongo Vence Guerra*, referring to a manifested quality of the mpungo Nsasi, hence nkisi. In most cases when a palero speaks of *his Zarabanda* or *his Mama Chola* it is in reference to the nkisi – but this implies of course the mpungo, or rather set of mpungos, it takes its unique quality from. This distinction is important to realize, as it is here that we find the metaphysical implications inherent in Palo Mayombe. Given Palo Mayombe's practical and personal nature these aspects are often ignored in favor of the importance of the spirit bond itself. I do however believe it is important to realize these distinctions as it contributes to a greater understanding of the traditional premises found at the core of the cult. Palo Mayombe is about making earth and death come alive, it is necromantic sorcery at its most refined. The resurrected dead are commonly resurrected within a divine setting, being subject to the creative powers of Nzambi in man and within mpungo. The mpungo represents a spiritual reality, the natural truth behind the idea of the nkisi. Mpungo are the powers that move the world in conformity with creative choice and action. The result of these actions and choices manifests in the guided gathering of items of the world of matter that upon being infused with life and breath will manifest a distinct idea born from the possibilities held by Nzambi. Some people have seen it opportune to simply take this technology and apply it in modern systems of cult and magic. I would here advocate caution. Palo Mayombe is per se a religion, even if I tend to see it more in terms of a cult. With this I have in mind its unique focus and religious arboretum which sets it somehow apart from the contemporary social idea of a religion. Because of this an even greater care should be displayed in the way one seeks to borrow from this sacred province. Often modern occult actors seek to incorporate potent religious strategies in a personal occult system. However, Palo Mayombe is not a personal cult and its sacred province of lore is not subjective, but a divine modality teaching how to bringing divine life into unique representations of divine possibility within given parameters. As I see it, if one is not true to the core of the tradition and simply robs parts from it, one is being unfaithful to the tradition. If one makes dishonest claims they will automatically be repelled by the guardians of the cult. A truthful approach rests in understanding the cult or religion which one is borrowing from, and thus realizing that what one is doing is other and different. This is all rooted in respect, a sense of sacrifice and honor. Borrowings and exchange occurs when cultures meet and people meet, but mutual understanding – or at least an attempt of such – must be the foundation of this. Here we find the difference between synthesis and syncretism. The former being motivated by a natural sympathy that generates a wider horizon of agreement, while syncretism on the other hand is more a reflex of uncritical wishes imposed upon the subject matter. This is important to keep in mind as we now turn our attention towards the nkisi manifested as nganga.

The nganga is also known as *prenda*, which means price, precious or jewel, and also *fundamento*, foundation. It is the unique material representation of cosmic and terrestrial powers adorning the resurrected dead, the nkisi. From the perspective of a palero the idea encapsulated in the vision of the nganga is to give birth to an nkisi. This nkisi is always unique and is given a name and signature, symbolized by the firma, which makes part of the intimate secret between the Tata and his

nganga. Only the Tata knows the name and sign of his nkisi and as such
is the only one who can control it, by the intimate token of trust represented by the true name. This idea is quite similar to the importance
of knowing the true name of spirits in the Solomonic tradition and the
true name of G-d in Judaic mysticism. This same idea is also found in
Brazilian kimbanda where the titles of the spirits are just this – *titles* –
while the name proper is a matter of trust and dedication that is only
revealed over time.

The nganga can come in a great variety of forms. The forms most
well known are those utilizing terracotta or iron cauldrons with a skull
in the centre and circled by sticks. Others are given inside wooden fig-
ures, or what is properly a *Chicherekú* in the original sense. The nganga
can also be given in the form of a *macuto* or talismanic object made
from fur or leather, as a *mpaka* or horn, inside a human cranium alone
resting on a bed of earth, inside dry sticks wrapped in cords and fur
and even as a small cauldron containing all the items pulverized so it is
impossible to differentiate the *secret of the nganga*.

The nganga is composed of many levels; all of them carry deep meanings and direct powers. The cauldron itself, circular and solid defines
the world and womb of the nkisi. At times a chain is placed around the
cauldron which is interpreted in several different ways, but should be
both a token of securing the soul of the nkisi as well as being a memory
of from whence it came, the slave forged in chains. The various metals
used in the construction of the nganga are both a memory of the met-
allurgic heritage amongst the people of the upper Kongo, such as the
Akan, as well as being sacred representations of the powers of mpungo
as they manifest in stars and planets. The machetes are added to remind
us of the violence that is entwined in its history, to literally give the
nganga tools to defend itself and its owner with, and also to bring stability. The various forms of earths and liquids are all representatives of
a movement in nature or in social organization. Nothing is accidental.
If you want the nganga to have healing powers you will include dirt
from several hospitals, a doctor's clinic and whatever resonates along
this chain of sympathy and replicates the primal principle or point being worked. The sticks are of utmost importance, the sticks or palos

turn the womb of earth, fluids, and metals into a magical place – the forest of the hills of Mayombe. All African cultures conceive the forest as the place where the veil between the worlds is particularly thin and it is in the forest that initiations are commonly performed. It is here the visible and invisible powers can meet and interact. The woods must therefore be chosen on the basis of understanding which woods naturally draw which vibrations and energies. The bilongos or macutos are magical charges that are added to the nganga and make a specific type of prenda, for instance a Nsasi. In addition to this, bones are essential. The knowledge of how to assemble the prenda is naturally bound by oath, but I believe it is possible to go quite far in describing the secrets without breaking one's word. This is possible because the true secret of Palo Mayombe lies in the blood of the lineage. It is the ancestors of the rama that carry powers to and fro and without this element the creative link of understanding and power is not in place and thus the prenda will not be infused with the ancestral chain that all prendas are ignited by. The initiatic chain is what sets the palero apart and it is from this that the creative powers of Nzambi are enabled.

The nganga is a delicate jewel to construct and takes a minimum of one month to assemble, if done properly. It is hard work for the Tata because legions upon legions of mpungo, nkisi and nfumbi will walk and speak with the Tata during this time. It is absolutely essential to make a vital and fluid connection with any object brought to form part of the prenda as it is important to connect with every item made inside the prenda. I cannot stress this enough, but this vinculum is of lineage. It is through the lineage, the rama, that this ability unfolds naturally and it is through this ability that the Ngangulero demonstrates that he is truly what he aspires to be. Many claims to be paleros, but in the end spirit gives the grace that effectuates this claim. The prenda is not simply a tool subject for a raw magical technology, it is the bringing together of a new member of ones family. The prenda is known by the name of a man or woman who once walked the earth – it is not necessarily a direct work with mpungo, it is a work of the skull – *kiyumba*. As such it cannot be mistaken for any form of conjuring or summoning of spirits, it is something different, as I have clearly demonstrated in the

previous chapter. Perhaps it is better if we think of the prenda as com-
posing a body for a soul to live within. This means that ideas of creating
'astral ngangas' has no root in the reality of Palo Mayombe and cannot
be taken to reflect its mystery in any way. Any modern theosophical
reading imposed upon Palo Mayombe is a disturbance of its traditional
coherence. The essential parts of the prenda resonate with the faculties
of the body and even the abilities latent in humans which we often
deny, such as bi-location and astral travel.

All prendas need the *matari*, which is the thunderstone. The matari
can be an actual thunderstone, that is a stone in the shape of an ax or
the fulgurites, but virtually any stone can be generated and endowed
through rituals to serve as the matari. The matari is the seal and solidification of the prenda. It represents the power of Nsasi and Nzambi to
create life, and at the same time it is the solidification of life-force and
corresponds with the nature of the bones. Seashells must make part of
the prenda as this is not only nkisi that brings abundance and money,
but also because the solidification of abundance they represent. Feathers are added in conformity with the nature of the prenda, and always,
absolutely always Mayimbe, the vulture, must be present. If no other
feather is to be found at least you need to have Mayimbe and thus a
deep connection to the mystery that gives spirit wings is established.
Many prendas are also given with an *mpaka nganga* which is the prenda
in miniature. The *mpaka* is the horn of a bull, ram or buffalo filled with
the same contents as the prenda and sealed. In this way you can easily
carry the prenda with you to different locations. Another horn can also
be prepared, which is the *mpaka vititi*. This mpaka serves as the eyes
of the prenda and is the vinculum that makes divination exceptionally
accurate. Through this mpaka the nfumbe/nkisi sees the world and on
the basis of the mysterious connection between the worlds of death
and nkisi it gives counsel. A prenda also needs several *macutos*, these are
charms/talismans that carry a particular virtue, much like special skills
you want the prenda to possess. It needs *bilongo* which in reference to
the prenda means workings, that is a particular magical solution which
is introduced into the body of the nfumbe. There are also *mpolos*, a
great variety of powders, and indeed some prendas can be made up

solely from mpolos. Though not a prerequisite it is also good to give to the prenda an *mpolo nan* also known as *Sese*, the companion of Gurunfinda. Sese in Palo Mayombe is seen as similar to the Yoruba Aroni, the dog-headed servant of Gurunfinda. This is a macuto that calls the spirit of the forest and enables work with the wilderness, it should be carried on your body and sacrificed to upon entering the woods when gathering the sacred palos or wooden sticks.

Some lineages, like the Changani, also segregate *Chicherichu* as a separate part within the prenda. Chicherichu is usually a wooden image that isolates the ndoki part of the prenda. Chicherichu is represented by maggots and termites and the decay of offerings left in the munanso. It represents the nefarious parts of man, what is aggressive and tense and it carries great protective potency.

The palos, the bilongos and the nfumbe itself is essential for generating the nganga. You do not have a prenda without these items. Equally important, to make a complete cross, is the *mati mati* or the heart of the prenda. This is the first thing made for any prenda. Its construction is simple, but the operation is secret. I can say that it involves the heart of a chicken or rooster sacrificed to the mpungo which you want to beat inside the body of the nfumbe.

The first task in making a prenda is to gather the secrets of the mati mati upon the firma of Lucero Cuatro Vientes, (Lucero of the Four Winds) which happens to look pretty much like the Yowa, and erect the central pillar. The central pillar is a prepared piece of the Ceiba which serves as the axis for the descent of the spirit. Some ramas, like mine, make a triad of bilongos around the central pillar and from here the Nkuyo is invited to lead the construction of the nfumbe's body. Nkuyo is always the first and fundamental principle, not because he is a divine linguist, but because he leads the herds of nfumbe and nfuri through the treetops. He is the mercury of Palo Mayombe.

In all this various forms of lustral waters are needed, like *chamba* – which is a fiery drink made from a base of aguardiente, gunpowder, spices, bones and peppers – and herbal infusions and potions often blended with dry white wine, a drink as sacred as the aguardiente, given its sacredness to Cobayende, the Boneherd.

At the heart of Palo Mayombe we find the *nfumbe*. Even in the most spiritual of the Kimbisa orders we find its presence, at least in the form of *mpolo nfumbe*, bone dust.

The need for a whole corpse or even a whole cranium is a myth, although it provides a more solid connection with the nfumbe. Actually, it is possible to invite the presence of one of the conscious dead to rest in the nganga with less than this. The main focus is in the contract made with the nfumbe and from this interaction a great variety of re-animations can take place.

There are various types of exhumation that can be performed. There is the exhumation proper of the corpse, parts of the corpse, symbolic exhumation and exhumation of bones that have previously been ex-humed. The essential idea is to reveal the nfumbe and interact with him or her with the object of forming a contract. The nfumbe must be willing to be seated in a new body and to become part of your house-hold. Defying this principle can lead to occurrences of *nfuri*, the rest-less and malevolent dead, or simply failure. The contract takes the form of purchasing the soul of the nfumbe. The underlying idea here is that the soul has engraved its memory and qualities upon the bones. When the bones are reanimated the virtues are once again brought to life. You will pay for the soul with tobacco, aguardiente, gunpowder, coffee, candles, money and blood. This must be left in place of the nfumbe as a price paid to Cobayende and Centella, the owners of the boneyard. Clearly there are many references to god-making strategies and more nigromantic and necromantic operations at play here. But this work is always focused on bringing to life an ally, a family member into the existing fold – and this does bring some interesting complications and marvellous levels to our ideas of ancestry, revenants and ghosts.

THE ORIGIN OF THE PRENDA

The historical origins of the prenda have been discussed, but in Palo Mayombe Brillumba we also find a mythical account about the first nkisi which is equally important. This myth relays both literally and by allegory the inner secrets of the nature of the nkisi and it also makes evident the importance of Mayimbe (the vulture) in the cult. Here is the story presented with no futher interpretation given, those who hath eyes to see will see:

Once upon a time in the land of Brillumba was born Mambe, child of Murabanda. This happened in the land of Nkita. In Brillumba lived a tribe known as Lumboma. Murabanda was a great hunter and respected sorcerer and one day he took his son who was at this time called 'mountain', to the wilder parts of the mountains. Here he taught him all the secrets of sorcery and all the secrets of the wild he knew, telling him that he was to take his place upon his eventual passing. In memory of his father, Mambele, Murabanda named his son Mambe.

Murabanda had also another son, Barabanda. Barabanda, loved the solitude of the wild terrain in the mountains and grew up to be a strong and skilled warrior whom at young age lost himself to the mysterious call of the forest. Barabanda in the prime of his youth gave death to his tribesman Mariquiri in combat and this act gave tongue to the revelation that Mariquiri's wife, Mariwanza, was having a secret affair with Barabanda.

A council of warriors and tribesmen were assembled to form a court to judge Barabanda, because infidelity was punishable by death. Aware of the danger he ran into the wild without leaving any tracks. He gave death to whoever entered the wild woods and found him. But Barabanda kept watch over his people and each time his tribe fought with cannibals he was there, fighting at their side dressed the skin of the Ngo (leopard). He fought hard and nobody could defy him. He carried at all times the mpaka (sacred horn of vision) of Mambele, his grandfather. Through it he could orient himself and see what was going on. He was regularly feeding the mpaka with the blood of Ngo. Murabanda, his

father, had at all times used the drums to call his people and he knew
the keys to call each and every one except for the key to call Barabanda,
which he had forgotten. Alas he could not speak with him. He had the
keys of the drum from Lowanda, Marocuto and Gangalewga that were
given as gifts in the sacrifice of white men to the leopard. The sanctity
of the leopard came to be such when the deceased Mambele, at a young
age found under the work of the lightning a young leopard shivering
from cold and fear at the side of his mother who had been struck by
the bolt. Mambele took Ngo and raised him in a cave where he grew
into maturity by his side. Ngo was his favorite and Mambele took him
as his protector against the forces of nature. In the cave of Mambele,
Ngo learned to know and nurture a deep relationship with Murabanda.
Ngo received honors often and was fed regularly, especially at Easter,
when he received human sacrifice. This was a secret ceremony. Every
time Ngo was attended to with sacrifice his roar was heard over the land
causing great awe amongst the tribesmen. But with time the vigor of his
roar became weaker. The weakness of Ngo was mirroring the state of
the dying Mambele who in his fading state urged Murabanda to gather
the wisest of warriors to come to the cave to help Ngo. Mambele sensed
something horrible taking shape. Murabanda called Nbako, Sakilande,
Enkarime, Wariani, Entumbirona and Mambe who were the strongest
and wisest men. They were the ones who would participate in the investigation. They all knew that the future of the tribe depended on the
safety of Ngo. They went to the cave and found Ngo dying and there
they prayed until he gave up his spirit. Mayimbe (vulture) knowing his
role in the halls of death was circling in the air making his funeral rites,
preparing to consume Ngo's rotting flesh.

They placed the remains of Ngo in a calabash and closed it with a
stone. He was dead but continued to serve as a sign of prosperity for
those faithful to nature and his grandson. In order to keep the spirit of
Ngo strong even in death one had to give to him offerings. The strongest and most cunning was Mambe who voluntarily offered himself to
serve as the sacrificial victim, but in spite of his offer a divination was
made. The divination told them to go to the river and gather seven
stones. They went to the river and brought seven stones. The carrier

of the stone that looked like the tongue of Ngo would be the victim. The carrier of this stone was Mambe. Murabanda in silent acceptance placed a blindfold on his son and Mbako was elected to be his executioner. Mbako had refused this role due to their deep friendship, but he was not heard. Malongo wanted Mambe because he would be nkisi...

Enkarimi and Guariere guarded the roads to the ritual since the ritual had to be kept secret from the rest of the tribe. Sakelande did the markings where Mambe was to be placed and prayed to Malongo (the tornado/*remolino*) since he was about to be made nkisi. They made the three signs of the sacrifice, life and death of Mambe. Sakilande, the messenger wore the palo of ebony that was hardened in the fire in such a way that it served as a machete. Those at the right of Mambe would bring the special gifts, which were the head of the Caiman alligator, wax, water from the fountain, honey, the Oromandiao bird (wind bird), a coconut, 21 coins, a thunderstone, seven river stones and the burning palo (*palo fuerte/brazo fuerte*) that would replace the candles. A serpent, a vulture, the egg of a vulture, the three drummers, symbol of joy and will, the weapons of a warrior, symbol of courage and strength, cowry, symbol of abundance, seawater as symbol of greatness and mystery, well water as a symbol of depth of earth, yam, corn and plantain, were the 21 rights/fees that Mbako presented. Murabanda was distanced and Entumbiroma made his entrance carrying chains to secure Mambe and therefore make his pain more slight. He was strangled by the chains and decapitated by the machete. Slowly the blood began to run and the first seven droplets fell, so mother earth received her rights first. Doing this they declared to nature that they were without fault, but rather that the chains and machete were to blame for this. This being done they separated the kiyumba (head) of Mambe from his body and removed his heart, genitals, feet, hands, tibias and liver. The liver was delivered to Sakilande, who took it to a place for Mayimbe to eat as payment for the ceremony. Since Ngo started to show the signs of death Mayimbe was always around. It was necessary to hide the body of the dead leopard and give it to Mayimbe to eat away from the place of ceremony so she would not be able to find where the body was hidden. The Kiyumba of Mambe was carried by all, after smearing their hands with honey and herbs so the blood would not taint them. They placed the kiyumba together with Ngo who was in the calabash veiled in wax, together with the egg of Mayimbe which had also been sacrificed as payment for his inopportune gift. The egg served as token of life and birth. His entrails were placed inside a Palo cana brava together with those of Ngo, making it a sacred attribute. With the decapitation of Mambe and the death of Ngo (symbol of the talking drums) the tongues were brought together with seashells so Mambe (symbol of divination/talking though shells) would speak with the voice of Ngo and be able to talk through the chamalongos. The conjoined tongues were then consecrated by the tongue and the head of a talking bird (parrot). The feet of Mambe were buried by Sakilande at the foot of the stone where the calabash of Ngo with his Kiyumba and the Kiyumba of Mambe were placed. Entumbirona then severed the toes from the feet and gave them to Sakilande who buried them in a particular place where the four winds meet and summoned the winds. In this way he secured and sanctified the place of Mambes execution and made it possible for Mambe to walk in the directions of the four winds. They then took the tibias and made from them a cross in front of the stone where his calabash was resting so the 'leopard-man' would walk only when authorized, since crossing the tibias would hinder his movement.

With a piece of Mambe's heart the other fees were prepared as an *ankuta* (macuto) and turned into food for the Caiman and the snake. Since Caiman does not speak and snake does not sleep, they would guard the secret. The Caiman was then offered as a companion of sacrifice, because he is ngando batalla, or 'point of fight', by virtue of his antiquity and strength. Mighty dweller at the river, first ngando became the guardian of silence. The rest of the 21 items were given to the earth in sacrifice.

The founding legend of the Carabali Abakuá society carries some interesting similarities with the founding myth of Palo Mayombe Brilluma. The Abakuá myth exists in several versions, which are variations on a theme. The myth tells of Sikán, a princess or noble woman who at the river catches an odd amphibian fish like creature. This creature is Obon Tanze, the reincarnation of a Leopard society king. He is noted by his voice, his roar. Sikán unknowingly catches 'the voice', *ekue* (symbolized by a drum and a drum beat), and witness to this act is Nangabión, the serpent who fell from the crown of the Ceiba (the silk cotton tree, *Ucano Beconsi*). The sorcerous warrior Ekuenón also sees Sikáns' capturing of the voice, a most prized possession. He tells this to Sikáns father who orders her secret execution. What transpires is a transformation of Sikán where she becomes the womb that holds the voice of Tanze. By finding the secret she appoints herself as the unhappy gift that makes possible Tanze to be nkisi. Tanze is deeply related to the Abakuá drums and it is here the mesmerizing voice of the leopard is sounded out and induces inspiration and prophetic reverie.

This is a very superficial recounting of a myth with many intricate layers, and through them multiple mystical codes, but the basic idea is similar to what we find in Palo Mayombe in terms of how the fundamento is gathered and receives life. The relationship Palo Mayombe has with Èkpé societies, leopard societies, in Central Africa is worth pointing out, but we will stay true to the Creole focus of this work.

I have chosen here a dozen mpungo/nkisi considered to be the most popular and widespread of the powers that are utilized to give birth to the nganga. These twelve taken together are able to summarize a complete sorcerous field of interaction, almost a zodiac of Palo Mayombe. Here we find the wind, the earth, the waters and the mountains and the great variety of qualities and the spiritual gifts they give to the Ngangulero. I have given *mambos* (songs) for each one of the spirits and I have also in relation to some minkisi presented formats of ritual working.

The focus in this section is on the linguistic roots of these nkisi and mpungo. I will then softly mirror them against the saints, as this is the image of apotheosis used in Africa and thus transported in the New World. I will strive to present in a simple and direct way the essential nature of these spirits as they were understood in the first synthesis with the Western World. In doing this I believe it is possible to present the mpungo/nkisi and their world in a way more true to the unique spiritual quality they possess and represent.

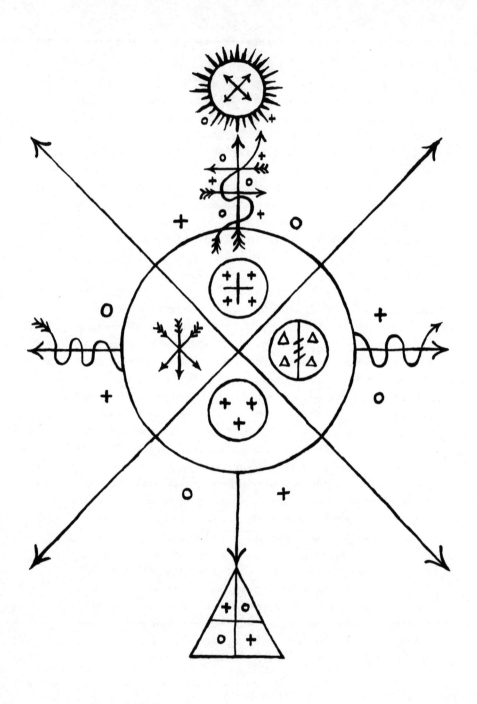

THE MYSTERIES OF LUCERO

Lucero is a crucial nkisi in Palo Mayombe. Some think that due to his name, light-bringer, that he is an invention. But this is not so, rather, his Cuban name precisely reveals his original function, as the spirit who sparks communication between the veils of the worlds. In the name Lucero is also revealed an African and European belief that sparks of light in the night represent, or truly are, spirits crossing the earth and air. The phenomenon of lights sparking around the treetops and descending on the crown of the tree is especially connected to pine trees and bamboo. These sparks of light are Nkuyu and the legion of dead ones following him. Nkuyu is an errant spirit who resides in the forest; it is the wilderness and the treetops that are his domain. This is the principle behind Nkuyu Nfinda, denoting the sparkling arrival of spirit upon earth, the breach between the invisible and visible world. Nkuyu carries a variety of meanings, depending on context and can signify *the soul of a diseased one, a shadow, a specter* and *a ghost*.

The proper Kongo name for Lucero would then be Mpungo Luufu Nkuyu meaning *the power of the errant spirit* or Nkuyu Nfinda, *the ghost/ ancestors that live in the wild forest*. Nkuyu can also mean *ancestor* in a great variety of ways, so we might say that Lucero is the power that carries the force to break down the veil between the visible and invisible world. Nkuyu is said to live in the woods, preferably in the treetops and of them, bamboo is his favorite dwelling place.

It is not uncommon to see *the errant spirit* conflated with myths such as those of the Lucumi Eshu and Santeria Eleggua, but this is at best an approximation and one that does not convey the rightful autonomy needed in understanding Lucero and his nature. Some ramas see in him St. Peter and others St. Norbert, but the most accurate correspondence in terms of saints would be Anima Sola del Purgatorio, Anima Sola or Anima Solas, the lonely souls in purgatory. These correspond to Nkuyu or more correctly, Kikuyu by being a legion of errant souls which are in-between. The purging flames of purgatory speak of the fiery nature of Lucero and harmonize with Nkuyu as an errant spirit who manifests in the sparks of spirit light around the treetops. Being of this errant nature he traverses every path and any road. Understanding Lucero on the basis of his saintly mirror give an interesting spiritual essence that makes *The Divine Comedy* of Dante a sort of testament to the world of Nkuyu.

Personally I have also found him to have a great affinity with the form and essence of St. Thomas and St. Anthony de Padua, even though St. Anthony is known by another name, Cuye Lumbembe. Cuye Lumbembe is considered to be the spirit who discovered Nkuyu Nfinda in the form of *the dead of the four winds*, but rather than the sparks of light he is the light within the lightning and became considered a form of St. Cyprian. St. Anthony was at times considered the second Christ and from this originated the Angolan movement known as Antonianism that took form in 1704 in Kongo through the prophetess Beatriz Kimpa Vita. St. Thomas is an interesting power to bring into the equation. For the explorers that discovered Africa this was the saint that paved the way to the Promised Land, for the Africans he became the portal of doubt and unknowing. Faithful and unpredictable, doubting even with his hands in the wounds of Christ, this is his nature, and these are the qualities also divulged in the function of Lucero.

By looking into the saintly mirrors and what they in essence represent I find that a more truthful perception of the mpungo and nkisi reveals itself. This might be rooted in the fact that the saints were understood to be nkisi by the Kongolese, and as nkisi a 'heathen' perspective on the saints was likely to be retained. A saint was manifesting a given divine quality with its lessons and qualities – just like an nkisi. Thus the words became synonymous.

For Lucero, the sparks from the blacksmith's forge are sacred, as are the dragonflies and the fireflies. Everything phosphorus that ignites life is his, the sulfur is his. He is *lucifera*, the pure experience of sensual matter, and therefore he is not exactly he, but she – and here enters the mercurial element that made the syncretism with Eleggua and Eshu such a viable, though erroneous, conclusion.

Lucero is the sulfur that opens the mouth and releases oracles. It is the sulphurous fumes in the mountains of Delphi that give augury and images to nature. It is the legions of errant spirits that walk the treetops and bring herds of spirits following after his tail. This is Lucero, a spirit of the wind which brings the beings from the other side to speak and manifest.

In order to effectuate his *mumia*, or corpse, you will need *ntoto* from the four corners of a hill which possesses the presence of death. You will need sticks and mpolos that carry the power of wind, wilderness and errant messengers, you will need sulfur and mercury and the tongue of a rooster. He needs feathers of various birds, and of those in particular ominous birds, such as vulture, raven and owl. The *mati-mati*, or heart of the prenda, is often sealed inside bamboo or a seashell.

His *firma* or signature is often recognized as three arrows descending in flight, signifying his power of bringing things from above to below. He is also depicted by the cosmogram, the cross and circle denoting his fundamental importance and necessity.

He can be made from a cement head or a bamboo stick, but most ramas make him in a cauldron of iron or terracotta. These Lucero's can be made to serve different purposes. A Lucero Malongo is usually given as a talisman and serves as a guide for the person. This Lucero is akin the Lucero de Guia or Guiding Lucero, but there is a more direct implication within the works of Palo Mayome. There is also the Lucero Kini Kini made in wooden statues. They are considered ndoki and similar to the Chicheriku – if not identical. There is also Lucero Guardeiros which lends much power from Zarabanda and is used to protect home and hearth.

Lucero takes its power from many places, for example: Palos from three different palm trees (*Benkosi*, *Membra* and *Butansake*). Ntoto Chola, Kalunga, *Nsambia*, Main Road, Market, *Kuana Finda*, Four corners, Highway, *Praza*, Cubayende, Rabbit, Rat, Chicken, Pigeon, Rooster, Mercury, Mayimbe, dry white wine, tobacco, aguardiente, and chamba.

Lucero is also known as: Tata Nkuyu, Tata Nfinda, Quicio Puerta, Maruga, Prima, Quatro Ventos, Vento Mundo, Orumbo, Numbe Nganga El Igualito, Mañunga, Lubaniba. There is also an nkisi called Mayunga that is directly related to Anima Sola on the path of Centella Ndoki that takes it's bilongo from Lucero and Mayimbe.

To speak with Lucero:

> *Aquiri nkutu guiri ndinga mpangui enbua oe nchila mati*
> *Com licencia to lo nfunmbe*
> *Que cuenda munanso kongo*
> *Ingenion la asunción*
> *Licencia Lucero*
> *Licencia Nganga Bendicion Padre Kuenda*

You can now continue with mambos (songs) or use the chamalongos to speak with Lucero.

Mambo Lucero:

> *Arriba la loma*
> *Arriba Lucero*
> *Que ya amaneció*
> *Arriba mi gallo*
> *Arriba mi gallo*
> *Ariba Lucero*
> *Arriba Lucero*
> *Que ya amaneció*

Mambo for beginning works with Lucero:

> *Abre Camino Pa Mayombe*
> *Abre Camino Pa Mayombe, Mi Nganga*
> *Abre Camino Pa Mayambo, Lucero*
> *Abre Camino A Sarabanda, Mayombe*
> *Abre Camino A NN*, Lucero*
> *Abre Camino Pa lo Buenom Lucero*

* *the name of your prenda/nfumbe*

Mambo for Lucero:

> *Yaya yayita, por el Sueto*
> *Lucero viene alumbrando Madruga*
> *Lucero prima Lucero Madruga*
> *Saludando a to los Npungos com Lucero Madruga*
> *Saludando a to loŝt Nfumbes com Lucero Madruga*
> *Ariva suena bajo el nfumbe com Lucero Madruga*
> *Diaka diaka nunca tecia com Lucero Madruga*
> *Piango Piango llega lejos com Lucero Madruga*
> *Ya recuerda Sacrifício com Lucero Madruga*
> *Yaya yayita, por el Sueto*
> *Lucero viene alumbrando, como e*
> *Prángana Lucero Prángana*
> *Pránana Mi nfumbe Prángana*
> *Buen Sueto Prángana*

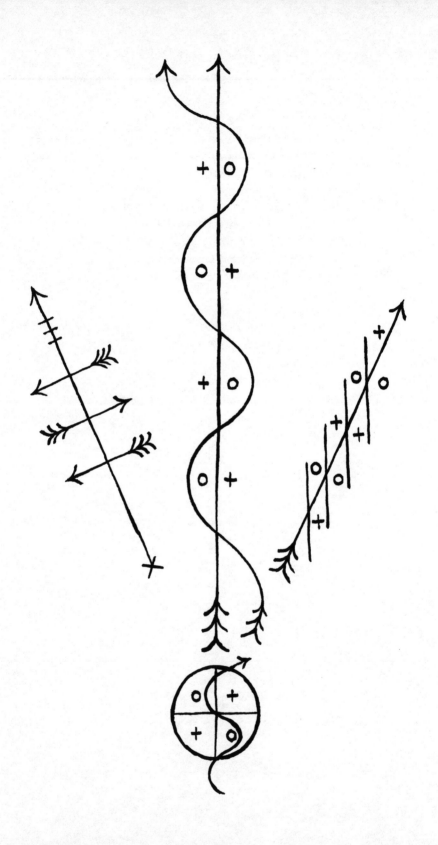

THE MYSTERIES OF ZARABANDA

Zarabanda is the most important nkisi in most ramas. He is the support, the stone the St. Peter of Palo Mayombe. His name is most likely from the kikongo *sála*, to work, and *bánda* which refers to something sacred or set aside, a taboo or a consecration.

Lydia Cabrera holds that the name derives from *Nsalaba*, which means to purify or discard unwanted elements, in other words exorcism. Yet another suggestion is that the name of this mpungo veils the secrets of *mumbanda*, which is a direct reference to the murmurs of the sorcerer, the prefix *mu* and *sala* which is before banda can also mean whispering. *Banda* in the context of work can also signify to forge, by the use of the hammer. The word *banda ntoto*, to forge the earth, is also a reference to initiation and to the bond that exists between blood kin.

It is quite natural that after Nkuyu or Lucero, Zarabanda takes on importance as the mpungo who works with the errant spirits. Zarabanda is the mpungo who forges what is errant into becoming steady and solid. Here Nkuyu is both the sparks and the fire, the very material Zarabanda is forging. We speak of creation as Heraclitus envisioned it. The metal worked is iron, traditionally assigned to the spine, from the spine all things became manifest, from the sacred bone known as Luz.

Zarabanda is also an historically important mpungo. Considering the Kongo and Bantu-speaking people's history concerning metallurgy and the wealth this brought them, any spirit presiding over iron, brass and gold would be seen as a powerful source of abundance. The sacred work, the banda might refer to metal working, from the most literal to the most alchemical and internal. The ability to forge hard substances and reveal their essence was to reveal the gold within, purified and perfect. To turn a chunk of metal into jewelry, statues and weaponry was a demonstration of the creative potential of Nzambi within man. In Cuba this power is found in the ritual of 'binding the four corners' which is basically a form of exorcism and binding of errant spirits made in order to perfect them. Zarabanda is the power of iron and fire – he is the force (*mpungo*) behind the blacksmith (*nkisi*). As such the mysteries of Zarabanda represent the essence of the mystery of creation. It is

Zarabanda who forges the errant spirits into nkisi. As the master of creative potential he also assumes the role as guardian of the laws that serve to preserve this potency. The same force that forges men also forges the sword, symbol of threat and order under the law of *kixila*, punishment.

Zarabanda is syncretised with St. Peter and St. Norbert in Kimbisa and in many other ramas with St. Michael the Archangel. These three forms speak well about the nature of Zarabanda: St. Norbert, an errant human and lover of the world and women, a knight and a courtier, a noble warrior; and St. Peter, the rock, the iron of the Church, fuse well in the image of St. Michael, the mpungo of purification and exorcism. This triplicity reveals the inherent nature of Zarabanda and through this why he is so important that many ramas give Zarabanda as your first or only prenda. St. Norbert is a knight akin to St. George and St. Jacques. It is the idea of the knight on the tracks of the stellar fields that replicates the essence of Zarabanda. Here we can even glimpse a form of transition between forging metals, and weapons and their use. The connection between the blacksmith and the knight is made evident in Zarabanda, he who makes matter sacred, who works sacredness. He is the *tronco mayor* in Palo Brillumba and as the owner of the *mbele*, machete, he is also seen as the blade who ensures that men behave in morally good fashion, since failing to exhibit good behavior will relocate you to his domain, in other words, the world of the bloodseeking mbele.

To build his mumia, you will need iron, 21 palos, horseshoes, machete, hair, a bone or the tooth of a horse, hair, bone or tooth of a dog, a snake and preferably its egg. A gathering of proper ntoto and macutos that connects him to the nfinda and the mountain must also carefully be introduced.

Zarabanda is also known as Salabanda, Brillumba Musi, Cuyere Ngando, Monte Oscuro and Yuyumbila.

Mambo for Zarabanda:

> *Sarabanda pé mañunga*
> *Sarabanda kimbisi kimbansa*
> *Sarabanda yo a ti rogando*
> *Sarabanda cosa bueno*
> *Sarabanda tu vititi*
> *Sarabanda cosa lindo*
> *Si hay malembo en los camino*
> *Sarabanda pé mañunga*
> *Sarabanda kimbisi kimbansa*
> *Sarabanda tu me güiri*
> *Sarabanda tu son cosa bueno*
> *Sarabanda yo a ti rogando*
> *Sarabanda abre camino*

Mambo for Zarabanda:

> *Zarabanda Cuye Nganga Cuye!*
> *Zarabanda Cuye; Yo te Quieron vê*
> *Zarabanda Cuye Nganga Cuye*
> *Zarabanda Son Mi Padre; Te Quieron vê*
> *Zarabanda esta en la Loma: Te Quieron ve*
> *Zarabanda esta en la Loma: Te Quieron vê*
> *Zarabanda esta en lo Monte: Te Quieron vê*
> *Zarabanda esta en lo Monte: Te Quieron vê*
> *Zarabanda esta en lo Mundo: Te Quieron vê*
> *Zarabanda esta en lo Mundo: Te Quieron vê*
> *Rayo pata a mi Mundo: Te Quieron vê*
> *Rayo pata a mi Mundo: Te Quieron vê*
> *Zarabanda son los vientos: Te Quieron vê*
> *Zarabanda son los vientos: Te Quieron vê*
> *Zarabanda cosa buena: Te Quieron vê*
> *Zarabanda cosa buena: Te Quieron vê*

Zarabanda Cuye...! Ya Son lãs Horas awe!
Zarabanda Cuye... te Estoy llamando Awe!
Zarabanda Cuye...! La rayo pata mundo awe!
Zarabanda Cuye...! Tu no me oyes awe!
Zarabanda Cuye...! Te estoy llamando awe!
Zarabanda Cuye...! Ya son...lãs horas awe!
Zarabanda Cuye Nganga Cuye
Zarabanda Cuye: Te Quieron vê
Zarabanda son Mi Padre: Te Quieron vê

THE MYSTERIES OF VENCE BATAYA

Vence Bataya is also known as Watariamba, from the kikongo *Wa tári a mbá* meaning stone of fire. Frequently, and correctly, it is possible to find Nkuyu as a prefix to the name, giving the meaning of *the errant spirit of the fiery stone*. In Briyumba this mpungo is considered to be the power of hunting and thus in Ochosi they see a reference to the camp fire as being the fiery stone. For the kimbisa this is St. Norbert. The association with St. Norbert is interesting as he was struck by lightning and fell from his black horse. While knocked out by the lightning he went through an inner visionary revelry and regained consciousness with a new sense of purpose. The courtier went to the monastery in Xanten, Rhien and accepted the ordination he had refused for years. His conversion was seen as dubious by many and Norbert's response was to donate all his property to the poor and become an errant preacher. After some years as a traveler he was ordered to found a monastic order. He founded his order in a remote valley of Prmontr using one of the strictest canons to regulate it. There are many aspects here that would ring true for the Kongolese. To be struck by lightning and survive would be like an immediate deification. The thunder represented Nzambi's creative spark, it was the fire of life itself. The wandering element and also the strictness of his canon would all make sense in light of the harsh and uncompromising nature of Vence Bataya.

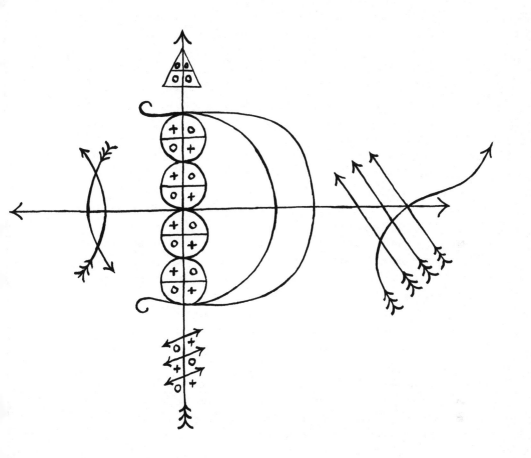

Watariamba is also named after his primary stick, Palo Fuerte, and is the tronco mayor of the rama Vence Batalla. His name is also related to *mbá* (fire) and *tarí* (the thunder stone). The burning stone might also be a reference to the molten magma at the centre of the earth and the laterite born from volcanic activity. If so, it is here we find a reference in temperament to the Yoruba Esu, and not in the form of Lucero. This is one of many examples of how faulty the syncretism between mpungo/nkisi and orisa can be. Vence Bataya is the power of the hunter. It is the mpungo that gives the gift of astral travel and holds the secret of the ntoto and mpolo of the wilderness. The powers of Palo Fuerte are particular present when the hunter approaches his prey in silence by merging with both the wild and the soul of the animal. This is also typical of how this nkisi executes work in the world, a fiery and silent surprise that strikes suddenly.

He is not only a spirit of the many facets of the hunt, but also of war and justice. In Palo Brillumba he is conceived of as having a pact with Zarabanda, the one who executes his potency. With the decline of the hunter's society Watariamba's secrets became even more veiled. Conceiving the power of justice as a factor implicit in the hunter and warrior mysteries would indicate that justice was seen in relation to the natural law and rhythm. It is the natural harmony which Vence Bataya is guarding.

The *tarí* or stone is an essential factor in West African cosmologies associated with creation. The stone symbolizes the matter that in meeting with fire generates the world. Vence Bataya is as such the creative impulse, the hot stone that generates the heat needed for Zarabanda to forge his weapons and the tools of both agriculture and the hunt. As such he is the meteorite and the laterite. He is the cold heat of the heavens and the scalding fire of the core of the earth that enables mpungo to descend upon earth and ignite life from above and below.

Given the complexity of his nature the construction of his *mumia* is also one of the more complex to bring to life. You will need a terracotta or iron pot, 21 sticks, feet and/or antlers of deer, arrows, and an iron bow. Matari stone, river stone, the burning stone and laterite. You will also need a rich amount of bilongos, Nsasi and a vast arsenal of mpolos in order to 'orient' Vence Bataya towards the realm of Gurunfinda as it is here in the wilderness and the woods that he is resurrected.

He is also known as Nkuyu Buenco, Saca Empeño, Lupokuyo, Santisi and Cabo Ronda.

Mambo to be used with Vence Bataya and also Zarabanda:

Abre La Puerta Nganga
Que Los Perros Ya Están Llegando
Los Perros Ya Están llegando Cabo Ronda
Los Perros Ya Están Llegando
Los Perros Ya Están Llegando Palo Duro!
Los Perros Ya Están Llegando
Los Perros Ya Están Llegando Mayombero
Los Perros Ya Están Llegando
Los Perros Ya Están Llegando NN†
Los Perros Ya Están Llegando
Los Perros Ya Están Llegando Kimbiseiro!
Los Perros Ya Están Llegando
Los Perros Ya Están Llegando mi Lucero!
Los Perros Ya Están Llegando
Los Perros Ya Están Llegando Cabo Ronda

† *Name of nfumbe*

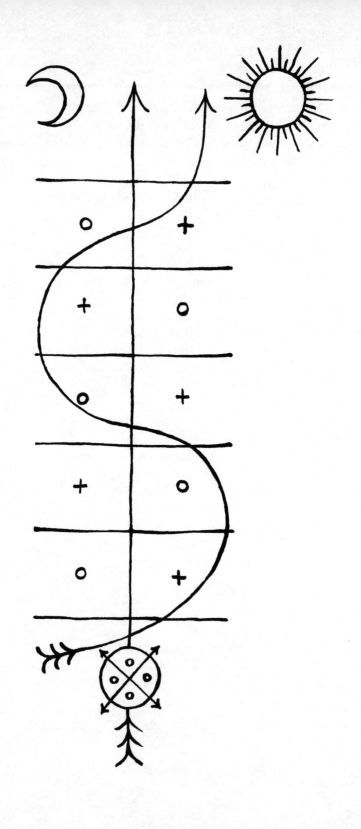

THE MYSTERIES OF NSASI/SIETE RAYOS

Nsasi or Nzázi means *lightning* and *thunder* and he is frequently known as Siete Rayos, *seven bolts of lightning*. He is the *fundamento* or tronco mayor in pure Palo Mayombe and in a great number of other ramas and munansos. Nsasi is considered to be the origin of pure Palo Mayombe. In Mayombe only one prenda is given. This prenda has the *nfumbe* as its focus, but Nsasi as the life igniting bolt of fire is the mpungo utilized in generating this form of nkisi. Since this nkisi represents the essential character found within the legend of the first prenda it is often considered ndoki. Palo Mayombe proper will build the Nsasi on the premise of the nfumbe. It is here we find a continuation of the original warrior cult's practice of beheading their enemies and reanimating them in the cauldron as a servant. The Nsasi in Palo Mayombe ramas will therefore be the resurrection of a specific soul on the prima materia of his skull and bones. This one prenda that you are given to work with is, from the perspective of many other ramas, considered to be more brutal than Nsasi given from other ramas. The skull is usually displayed prominentally, which many see as yet another sign of ndoki. Nsasi can also be given from other ramas and is adjusted in conformity with the rules of the rama.

Siete Rayos is together with Zarabanda the prenda that is most popular. In several ramas it is common to give either of these two, even if you are marked as possessing the qualities of another mpungo. His importance is vital in Palo as he not only represents the power of lightning, but also the Ceiba or the Royal Palm.

One of the first steps towards receiving the nganga is the presentation to the Ceiba. It is absolutely crucial that one is marked in front of the Ceiba and its spirit, Nsasi, blesses the path onwards for the Ngangulero. The palm tree stretches towards the heaven in a stout and erect manner and as such Nsasi represents the axis mundi of Palo Mayombe. He is the secret placed at the bottom of all prendas in the form of a small erected pole over the firma of Lucero. In most African societies thunder and lightning is considered a theophany and when it strikes, the place or object is immediately transformed into a powerful divine representation, touched by Nzambi. This view of thunder and lightning is not too different from the Roman idea of Jupiter, which is reflected in the large number of kings throughout Africa's history that formed cults to a deity associated with thunder and lightning. Nsasi lives in all forms of fire and can as such be seen as the very principle that enables creation and movement. In the kingdom of Kongo he was seen as having an affinity with Mukiamamuilo or Sta. Barbara. In Cuba this led to syncretism between this saint, Nsasi and Shango. Mukiamamuilo in Kikongo means the *grandeur of the head of the nobles* and refers to the crown earned by nobles and aristocrats in the time of Portuguese infiltration in the larger district of what they called Kongo. Nsasi is divine potential manifested in similar ways to Zarabanda. Whilst Zarabanda works the fire of creation, Nsasi possesses the flash of life.

His mumia replicates the activities of the thunderstone, the *matari*, which represents the power to give life, as does the sap of the pine. He is born by the powers of fire birds, like the phoenix and thunder birds, like raptors (and of those especially the eagle). He does need something of the cat or lion and the Ceiba. These are the powers that animate the nfumbe. He will need *ntoto* from a great variety of places and one of those must be mpolo from a tree struck by lightning.

Other names given to Siete Rayos are: Ngundo Liri, Siete Rayo Barremano, Siete Loma, Siete Brillumba Ngo, Siete Palma, Insasi, Nkita, Nkitán Kitán, Kanbaranguanje and Insancio.

Mambo for Nsasi:

> *Ahora veras*
> *Ahora veras*
> *Siete rayo en la palma*
> *Ahora veras*
> *Siete Rayos de mi confianza*
> *Y ahora veras si te rayo em la palma*
> *Ahora veras*
> *Piango Piango llega lejos*

Y ahora veras si te rayo em la palma
Ahora veras
Ahora veras
Ahora veras com Livencia de cuatro ensila
Ahora veras
Abre kutu NN[‡]
Y ahora veras, ahora veras si te rayo en la palma
Ahora veras

THE MYSTERIES OF TIEMBLA TIERRA

This mpungo is of great importance and is one of the more mysterious of the mpungos. The Bantu name for Tiembla Tierra is Máama Kengue, Máma being a title of veneration, while Kengue, from the Kikongo kanga, means *to bind* in the sense of pacifying. We might say that the name expresses the idea of *mother who pacifies*. This mpungo is said to dwell on the mountain top and is also known as *the earth shaker*. Tiembla Tierra is also related to the mpungo Nkita Kinseke or Nkita Minseke which in Kikongo can mean *the spirit of mountain* as well as *the spirit of the savannah*. It is seen as the counterpart to the watery spirits such as Nkita Kiamasa and Nkita Kiamamba. The Nkita Minseke spirits are spirits of mountain, wilderness and air with an affinity towards water. There is a relationship here with the Simbi class of spirits in Vodou and clearly Tiembla Tierra is a serpentine power resting within the mountain and the savannah.

This spirit is essentially female, but often manifests in male forms. This speaks of a mysterious relationship where a male mpungo has been graced by the mothers. The mothers are the waters that molded the mountains. At the very least this suggestion will provide a clearer understanding of the intimate relationship the Kongo perceived between the waters and the mountain. Máama Kengue can therefore signify to be *bound by the mothers* or *brought to peace by the mothers*.

‡ *Name of nfumbe*

His palos are any thorn-free palm tree, cotton, oils and milk. He is what flows from the mothers. As the Lord of the mountain he is also acknowledged as possessing the power of prophecy and interaction with the divine. We can see in Tiembla Tierra the image of Moses as he ventures up the mountain to receive the commandments, splits the red sea and converses with fire, the source of creation. These parallels are very telling, and explain how the Kongo with relative ease accepted Christian mythology as it replicated the qualities inherent in the spirits they knew so well. Tiembla Tierra is syncretised with Virgen de Las Mercedes, like the Obatala of Santeria. It is important to understand that Tiembla Tierra demonstrates by this syncretisation his veneration for the powers that gave him the gift of prophecy. By accepting the icon of the Holy Virgin he is also replicating the grace represented by the mothers who in their generosity provide the waters for the sustenance of the world just as they favor the spirit of the mountain to be their embodiment and emissary.

The idea of peace and mercy also influences the state of mind of the prophet and the sage. It is the stillness of the mind that is the central idea, the power of pacifying the world of movement and provoking ascent.

The mountain represents victory, in Christian doctrine; to ascend the mountain is akin to entering Jerusalem, the grand symbol of peace and harmony. It was at Mount Hermon that the Savior went to Nzambi, and it was at the same mountain he would reappear. It is this idea we find in Tiembla Tierra, the spirit of divine peace and salvation that makes prophecy possible. As such the *nsusu nfinda* (pigeon) is his animal, divine messenger of peace and divine inspiration. Tiembla Tierra is akin to the mystery of the Holy Spirit.

His mumia is based on the thornless Ceiba and pigeon in combination with a great diversity of waters and stones, shrubs and woods from the mountain. He walks with the cotton drape serpent and worships the mercury bound in crystals.

Other names given to Tiembla Tierra are: Vioco Zambi, Moco Zambi, La Mile Matari Punta Loma, Yolá, Iña Naába and Yeyé – although Yeyé means *joy* and is sometimes used to address Mama Chola.

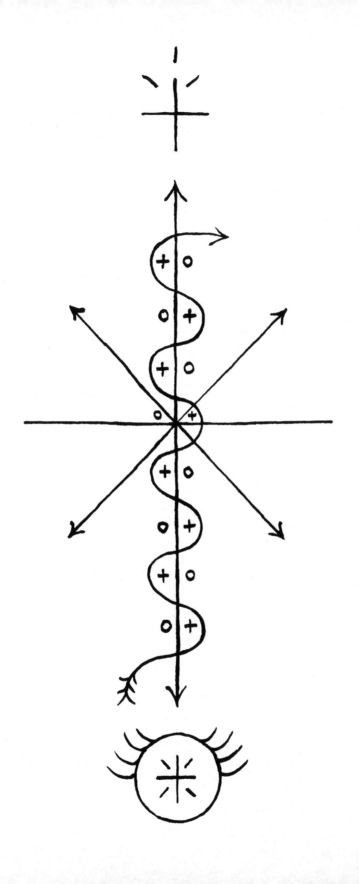

Mambo for Tiembla Tierra:

> *Tiembla Tierra Tiembla*
> *Pa que me llamas*
> *Palo Monte lo ma Sublime*
> *Palo Bueno ya son lãs hroas*
> *Ya son lãs horas Sala Maelco*
> *Sala Maleco, Malecon Sala*
> *NN§ Ya son las horas*

Mambo:

> *Estava durmiendo y sentia run run*
> *Estava durmiendo y sentia run run y*
> *Era Tiembla Tierra que vênia caminando*
> *Estava durmiendo y sentia run run*
> *Estava durmiendo y sentia run run y*
> *Era Tiembla Tierra que traia to lo bueno*
> *Estava durmiendo y sentia run run*
> *Estava durmiendo y sentia run run y*
> *Era tiembla Tierra que vênia com so nfumbe*
> *Estava durmiendo y sentia run run*
> *Estava durmiendo y sentia run run y*
> *Era Tiembla Tierra que vênia asi limpiando*
> *Estava durmiendo y sentia run run*
> *Estava durmiendo y sentia run run y*
> *Era Tiembla Tierra que vênia trabajando*

§ *Name of nfumbe*

THE MYSTERIES OF MAMA CHOLA WENGUE

The name Mama Chola Wengue is from the kikongo *ki yòla vwéngè*, *ki* being a prefix signifying plurality, *yòla* meaning falsity and *vwéngé* being the power that provokes confusion and dislike. She is syncretised with Nuestra Señora del Caridad del Cobre and Virgen de la Candelaria (also known as Mpungo Mama Wanga), but Mater Dolorosa perhaps fits better. Her syncretism with the orisha Ochun in Cuba is misleading. Chola is the painful judge of love. She is not the amorous love often associated with Ochun, but the element of conflict rather than desire. She is the jealousy and hatred that walks in shadow behind all forms of attraction and bonding. She is the dominatrix and the leather-clad love that is concealed in sadism and submission. She is reputed to be the power behind any confusion related to the feminine principle amongst any male spirit. We might see in Mama Chola the vilest tales of Aphrodite and Venus playing themselves out in the great field between nurturing and protection. She is love when it attacks the beloved, fraught with jealousy and anger. Here she shares features with Hera/Juno and Artemis. A successful relationship with her will always challenge the Ngangulero. Ruthless honesty must at all times be measured with impeccable integrity.

Mama Chola is also known as Mariquilla. Some see Mariquilla as a separate nkisi and others as a quality of Mama Chola. Mariquilla is the *bitter star of the river*. Her name can also be seen as connected to the Spanish pejorative *maricon* – homosexual – and thus suggests her critical sexuality as a power that does not conform to the social norms, but rather goes against the tide. Perhaps here we find an explanation for the great taboo against the induction of homosexuals in Palo¶ and the limitations on women – they represent a force too *cold* to handle. Her importance is great. In several ramas it is essential for the Ngangulero to be presented for Mariquilla even before the presentation to the Ceiba. It is as if the icy cold Mariquilla is the power that challenges and tempers on the road towards being born by fire in one's *rayamento*.

¶ Both this and infidelity were punishable by death or exile in Kongo. This prohibition was also carried to the New World, though not in nations of an Angolan origin, which were more liberal in terms of sexuality – an attitude we find present in its New World successor, Kimbanda in Brazil.

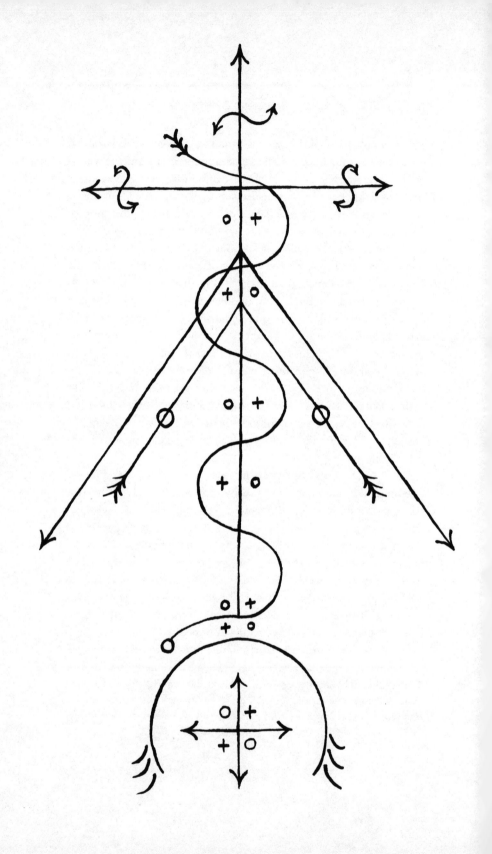

Mama Chola is the nkisi that carries the idea of the sinister typically assigned to the iconic witch. Mama Chola is the power of a vile and seductive woman who fondles you and excites you with great skill, always holding a dagger to the nape of your neck. She is the knife that runneth over with honey and blood.

To effectuate her mumia you need *mayimbe* (vulture) and *susundamba* (owl) and her most prized nfumbe is the skull of a prostitute or entertainer at the cabaret. She is honey and ice, the sting of bees and wasps. She is amber and she walks with crocodiles and alligators. The cobra coral is her friend. She needs copper, cinnamon and takes datura and belladonna as her plant allies.

She is also known as Chola Nguengue, Mariquilla Vence Guerrara, Ococo Marisela Ndoki, Duculango Zarabanda, and Chola Anguenge.

Mambo for Mama Chola:

>*Vuela mi Gavilán, Zunzún sin uñas*
>*Zunzún sin uñas, Zunzún sin uñas*
>*Vuela que vuela Zunzún sin uñas*
>*Vuela em el Zulu, Zunzún sin uñas*
>*Zâmbia te manda Zunzún sin uñas*
>*Vuela um Gavilán Zunzún sin uñas*
>*Arriba truena Zunzún sin uñas*
>*Vuela que vuela Zunzún sin uñas*
>*Va Piaco Piaco Zunzún sin uñas*
>*La Cuatro Nsila Zunzún sin uñas*
>*Lo Campo Nfinda Zunzún sin uñas*
>*Va pico loma Zunzún sin uñas*
>*NN** Zunzún sin uñas*
>*Vete a la Nganga Zunzún sin uñas*
>*Va arriba Ntoto Zunzún sin uñas*
>*Cara bateando Zunzún sin uñas*
>*Vuela que vuela Zunzún sin uñas*
>*Chola Mariquilla Zunzún sin uñas*

** *Name of nfumbe*

THE MYSTERIES OF CENTELLA

Centella is not a kikongo word, but a name given to the garden of blood and bones, the cemetery. The name has multiple meanings from *beautiful*, to *creeping* and *spark of light*. Her name is also used as a direct reference to the cemetery, which she owns. The addition of ndoki to her name would indicate that she is *the spark of light in darkness*, suitable imagery for a mpungo who owns the graveyard and hence all the sparks of souls flying around there. She is reputed to be the most dangerous of all nkisi, but this is not necessarily so. She manifests in the mysteries of the bat, great symbol of illumination for several Sufi *tariqas*. Torment and tornados are her most intimate manifestations. She has deep relations with the mysteries of Sta. Muerte and indeed she is Lady Death, the very garden of Lord Death, Cubayende. In Cuba it is common to perceive her as multi-coloured – but she also harmonizes with the traditional tripartite qualities we find in Africa where she is red, white and black as typifying the extremes of female manifestation. She is not only Sta. Theresa de Jesus, but she is also Sta. Theresa de Avila. She is the fortress of death – and death is the collective sum of ancestral wisdom – and herein she gives the gift of enlightenment.

The wind that turns into storm is in African faiths a sign of ancestral presence. In the winds we hear lost wisdom and in the storms this wisdom is vibrant and devastating. Here opens the field of the restless dead and thus she presides over the mysteries of lycanthropy and vampirism. She is the power of transition. Whether the transition is between forms as from man to beast or from living to dead, it is still a transition to something *other*. Centella is this wisdom. Because she possesses all the wisdom of the night and the secrets that avoid the light of day she is ndoki and her messengers are vipers and spiders.

To effectuate her mumia you will need bat, eyes of wolf, horns of bull and a knife or nine. A convent of *nfuri* enters her cauldron and the nine-fold pact recreates her garden of lascivious and lusting death that brings wisdom from the beyond and enables oracles of the most profound virtue.

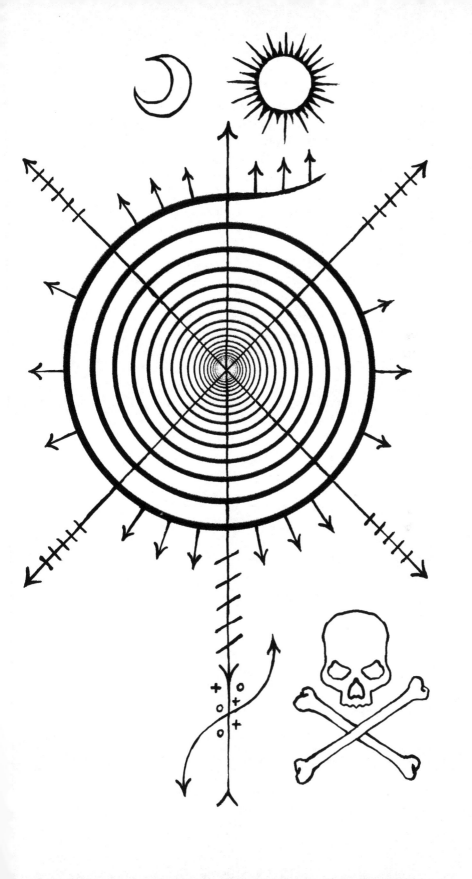

She is also syncretised with Virgen de la Candelaria, like Mama Chola, and she shares several other features with Mama Chola as she is also known as Mariwanga, Mama Wanga, Kariempembe, Yayá Kégue, Yayá Kéngué, Marufina, Maringoya, Mariaguairo, Tormenta, Adonque, and Remolino 4 Vientos.

Let us now look at the structure of a ceremony for Centella Ndoki, as this follows a liturgical structure applicable for most ngangas.

> *Temporal tumba palo come no tumba ojo*
> *Eh! Vamo allá Batalla Sierite la loma*
> *No digo Madiata Guiaguó guiaguo*
> *Varicoso dayo lindero cimbra ciguaraya*
> *Macreto bilongo … …*

Mark a cross with cascarilla in front of the nganga and say:

> *Chamalongo malongo chamalongo menanda*
> *Vengo com permiso de Nsambi*

The *nguyos* (godchildren) present will respond with:

> *Malemboé malemboé*
> *Bueno dia Prenda mia*
> *Arranca, que andamos mal*

You will then sing to her while you present *fula* (gunpowder) on her firma:

> *Intero ko ko ko nfinda ta*

Before igniting the fula you will sing:

> *Nsunga, nfula mbara*

You will then touch the prenda with both hands and sing the following until you connect with the prenda:

Santo Tomás ver y creer. Con licencia Nsambi, Con Licencia Siete rayos,
con Licencia Viejo Nkobo, Con Licencia Zarabanda.
Centella quita la yezca a todos los Santos. Nkisa padre Nsambi

Oration:

Carajo Zapatico yo quiero ver, manda que vea ojo!
Carajo, yo tá mirando a todo el mundo
Dia que to diga mentira la mar prede candela
Jarabata dumba consaya va subi loma
Tu arrastra cola en tiempo fangi
Tiempo seca to subi saya Yo quiero ver
Si hay Dio hay Dio hay Dio el mundo susta
Yo noa susta yo te manda tu responde
Ma rayo parta carajo yo quiere vé
Si tu no sive yo te bota si tu no camina
Yo te da candela yo te manda Mundo tiembla
Hay Dio hay Dio hay dio Zapatico
Malako dumba cons aya va subi loma
Santo Tomas ver y creer. Con Licecia Nsambi
Arriba Sambia abajo, con licencia Padre Nkisa
Padre Nganga, padre Nkuyo, con Licencia
Siete Rayos, primero Sambia que to la cosa...
Centella quita leka Mama busukú da licencia
Viejo Ekobo me acompaña, Elio el chino d alicencia
Buena Niche, buena noche Padre Nganga
Si son tarde, buana tarde, si son dia
Bueno Dia

With Centella it is also common to call the powers that support her presence, which is Lukankazi/Lungambe; this is subject to some particular details, but the mambo is:

Mambo Lungambe:

> *Lungambé no quiere a nadie*
> *Lungambé mato a su madre*
> *Lungambé mato a su padre*
> *Lungambé no tiene amigo*
> *Lungambé es gangulero*
> *Lungambé los Malos Palos*
> *Lungambé los Tronco Ceiba*
> *Lungambé los Tata Nfungue*

Mambo to praise the Nganga Ndoki:

> *Mi nganga son pañuelo luto*
> *Mi Nganga son kiyumban fuiri*
> *Mi nganga son lo indiambo*
> *Cifra Cifré mi tormenta*
> *Cifra Cifré ya son las horas mi tormenta*
> *Sambiampungo mal rayo parta*
> *Lo Zarabanda mal rayo parta*
> *Lo Tronco Malo mal rayo parta*
> *Mal rayo parta a Kiyumba Nkisa*

Mambo for Centella:

> *Aguara Aguara Andota*
> *Nguidoya Nguidoya*
> *Aguara Guindo Aguara Guindota*
> *Aguara Guinde Aguara Guindota*
> *Ya so las horas Guindo Aguara Guindota*
> *Aguara Guindota Aguara Guindota*
> *Aguara NN †† Aguara Guindota*
> *Aguara Centella Aguara Guindota*

†† *Name of nfumbe*

THE MYSTERIES OF BALUANDE

Baluande represents the embodiment of the mothers as they manifest in the waters. Baluande embodies the powers that made Tiembla Tierra possible. Through their interaction the wisdom of the mountains flows within the waters of ancestral memory. The etymology is difficult, but might signify *that which is on the surface* and *that which is most elevated*. This can be the surface resting on the Kalunga itself, the water-mirror, hence she is popularly known as Madre de Aqua or Mama Kalunga. The Kalunga is in particular the salty waters of the great oceans but is also the realm of death, or perhaps more properly Kalunga is the realm of active ancestry. The ancestors that continue to influence us are understood differently to the modern Western idea of the dead. Ancestors are found both in the waters and in the centre of the earth. The latter is in Kikongo called Kumangongo and though similar to Hades, we need to understand this as a good thing. A similar division of death is found in Nordic myths. Here we find two realms, one is relegation to the waters and the golden halls of Ran, while the other is Valhall situated in the centre of divinity. The latter is reserved for warriors and hunters, those who died in bravery and with honor. The kingdom of Ran was just as wonderful as Valhall – but Ran also gained dominion over the mysterious, and what was on the brink of the natural. The fact that the ocean does not produce but rather consumes light brings another important factor into the equation, and one which might explain the waters as the medium not for change and movement, but for transformation and metamorphosis.

Baluande is also known as Mpungo Kasimba, meaning *spirit that lives in the cavity of the waters*, clearly a reference to the occult and hidden virtues of water as it hides within the mountain. She is also Mbumba Mamba, *secret of the water* or *serpent of the water*, in the sense of fertility and abundance. The same idea is found in Nkita Kiamasa and Nkita Kuna Mamba. Her association with snakes and fertility seem to be the most salient aspects of her potency. It is an mpungo considered to induce stability and joy in ones life and brings riches, comfort and wealth. She is a tremendous force when it comes to altering one's for-

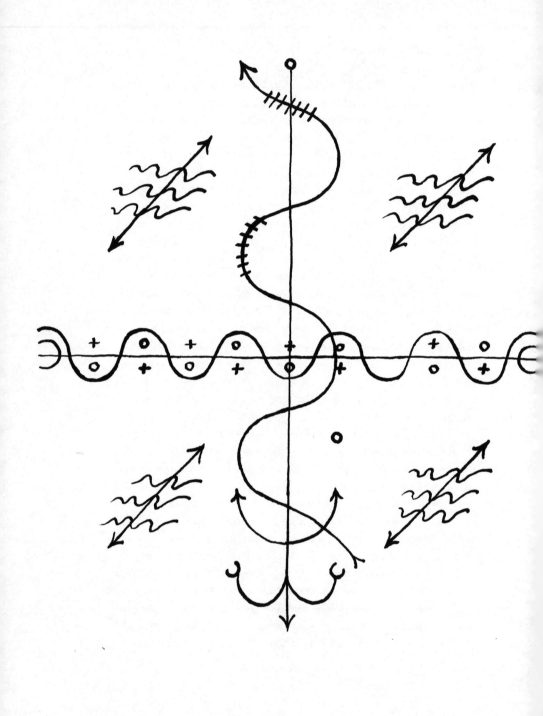

tune. This spirit is also referred to only as Mboma or Mbomba meaning serpent, boa, python (*mboma-ndongo*) and this tells us of the importance of both waters and serpents in African cosmology. Baluande is the power behind transformations on every scale, from turning a poor man into a rich man, to turning an unfavorable situation to ones benefit, to the Trans-Atlantic Crossing. This specter of manifestation testifies to her serpentine nature – which is one of secrecy and unpredictability. A serpent can never be really tamed, as the waters can never be tamed. Baluande gives riches freely and abundantly, but she is also the serpent that spins the wheel in the hands of Fortune.

As Mama Kalunga she was syncretised with La Virgen de Regla who in turn was seen as the orisas Yemoja and Olokun. She is the patron of sailors, fishermen, mermaids and mermen and all transitions and discoveries concerning water.

Her *mumia* is erected on swan, duck and serpent. Waters of all kinds are important as are all forms of ntoto carrying the idea of wealth and joy.

Other names given to her are Kalunga Mpaka Ndoki, Mayanguera, Patrón de los Congos, Bamba di Ngola, and Muana Lango.

Mambo Baluande:

> *Eriso Palo ande*
> *Omo de o hay juria engando de eriso Palo ande*
> *Vamos Engangar mama mia, como llueve*
> *Ngango Eta Correr*
> *Madre Aqua Awe*
> *Ngango Eta Correr*
> *Baluande Awe*
> *Mama Linda Awe*
> *Ngango estal llove*
> *NN[‡‡] eta Correr*
> *Mi culebra Awe*
> *Son anguila Awe*
> *Com tu maña Awe!*

‡‡ *Name of nfumbe*

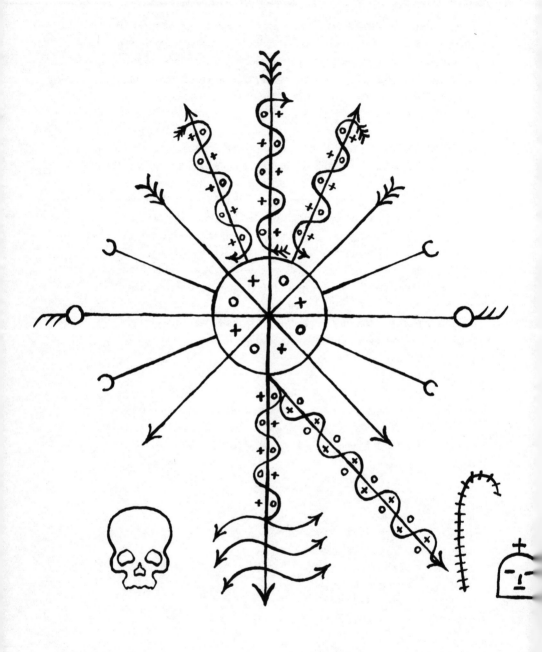

THE MYSTERIES OF COBAYENDE

Cobayende is Lord Death. He is the embodiment of death and resurrection in the flesh. Naturally he is the one who walks with Centella as his wife and daughter. By being the Lord of Death he is also the Lord of Earth, as this is the natural state of the body. Earth to earth he is the power behind all ntoto used to make the nganga alive. His name Tata Nfumbi or more correct Táata Mvúmbi means literally *Father/ Master of Death/Corpse*. This is not only a reference to him as Lord Death, but also to his reanimating powers. He is the earth that makes the mumia or corpse of the nganga, and it is only natural that Cobayende is syncretised with St. Lazarus, the one who was resurrected in the flesh, and thus possessor of the mystery of bringing life to what is dead. It must also be made clear that the St. Lazarus spoken of is not Mary Magdalen's brother, but the old man who feeds on the crumbs of the rich man's table in the biblical tale, leading to an experience of hell for the rich man. Both of these saints fit the image of Cobayende with their connection to the nefarious regions and the bone-garden. Nevertheless his mystery is closely knit and transformed through the coming of Pandilanga as the Kongo called Jesus the Nazarene, as it was through his intervention both Lazaruses were resurrected in *the bosom of Abraham*. The name itself, Pandilanga, means *divine father who was profoundly elevated*. To go to the nsulo, heaven, was uncommon, it was a mark of a noble king truly favored by Nzambi to *invert the way of thunder*. As such Pandilanga represented a divine anomaly that verified the natural order by the very fact of demonstrating the possibility of exceeding its natural borders.

He is also known as Mfútila which is the Kikongo name of St. Lazarus which means *powerful deity who attends to his sores*. It is here we find the affinity with the leprous man healed by Jesus Christ that received beatitude. The theme is both of resurrection and the sanctity of death. The sores speak not only of mortality being natural, but also of the phenomena of stigmata. In both instances Lazarus was laid to rest by bodily imperfections natural for the human condition, namely old age and leprosy. The importance of Lazarus, Magdalen's brother, is immense as he is the dead that returned to life, while Pandilanga who was the mpungo who resurrected him lost his body. These two mysteries are intertwined as a complete image of the resurrection. He represents the challenge of overcoming bodily infirmities and the transcendence occurring from this that connects man's spirit with Nzambi. He is the one who speaks of the frailty of the body and the strength of the spirit and the soul. It is Cobayende who is the guide of souls, the haven of peace at night. He can be understood as an ally of the Yoruba Omolu and the Vodoun Gede, but Cobayende's joy is never sexual, rather it is one of serenity, sensitivity and wisdom.

His mumia is made from parts of a complete corpse and palo muerto is his axis. He walks with dogs and vultures, and is the testimony to why vultures are so important in Palo Mayombe. The vulture is the watcher and also the selfless power that turns life into earth and enables new life to be brought forth. He is the crystal and all weeping trees, the veil and the coffin. Lustral waters of various kinds must be prepared and the sun and the moon must be united over his skull. As such he is the rose garden of pain and beauty, the garden of pleasure attained through death alone.

Cobayende is also known as Kumbaimbre, Tata Kañen, Tata Fumbi, Pungún Fútila. Pata en Llaga, Ndoki Yaya, Coralillo Ndoki and Marmol Blanco Dois Muletas and is considered a dangerous and demanding mpungo. His children are often made to receive Zarabanda or Nsasi instead of his prenda, given its grave-cold heat. Some say that it is not good to receive death on your head, but he is not death, he is the Lord of Death.

Mambo for Cobayende:

Yintiri Guao Guao Guao
Yinyiri Guao Mi Cobayende
Mi Cobayende va Campo Lemba
Yinyiri Guao Mi Cobayende
Mi Cobayende va Campo Nfinda
Yinyiri Guao Mi Cobayende
Mi Cobayende va Piaco Piaco
Yinyiri Guao Mi Cobayende
La mima Ngonda va cruzar Sulu
Yinyiri Guao Mi Cobayende
Va enterrar muerto va sacar vivo
Yinyiri Guao Mi Cobayende
Sacando Aqua ya va em canasta
Yinyiri Guao Mi Cobayende
Bajo el Tratado de lãs dos palmas
Yinyiri Guao Mi Cobayende
Ya va recuerda la sacrifício
Yinyiri Guao Mi Cobayende
Lo mismo Tata que manda na Congo
Yinyiri Guao Mi Cobayende
Vayamo Venga va Correteando
Yinyiri Guao Mi Cobayende
Na ma Camilio va escupe Sangre
Yinyiri Guao Mi Cobayende
Va como noca pa fiesta indemo
Yinyiri Guao Mi Cobayende
Mama Kalunga me esta llamando
Yinyiri Guao Mi Cobayende
Briyumba Congo son muy tratado
Yinyiri Guao Mi Cobayende
Soy Rompe Monte Soy Guinda Vela
Yinyiri Guao Mi Cobayende

THE MYSTERIES OF GURUNFINDA

Gurunfinda is the power that provides the materials that make possible the animation of the corpse. As such he is crucial, the life soaked matter which penetrates all parts of nature.

He is the Lord of the Greenwood, the secret resting in the sorcerous forest of the hills of Mayombe. Gurunfinda is invariably syncretised with St. Josef and St. Sebastian, of which the latter as well as St. John the Baptist and St. Ramon are clearly better reference points for his powers. He is the sap and blood of every tree, leaf and twig and he is the buzzing and humming of all insects.

In kikongo he is known as Sindaula Ndundu Yambaka Butan Seke. The name Sindaula means *to extract* or *to dry up*, Ndundu Yambaka, means *albino* or more correctly albino pigmy and Butá Nseke means *little man who is the master of the mountain*. The image generated is one of a spirit defying the social order, it is the wilderness that speaks through this short, white and dried up figure.

In Cuba the various parts of his name are all viewed as qualities or attendant spirits of Gurunfinda. This name is derived from the kikongo Ngúlumfinda, composed of *ngúlu*, wild hog, and *mfinda*, wild forest. It might appear that Gurunfinda is the supreme master of the wilderness while Sindaula and Seke are seen as his boar and dog-headed assistants. Gurunfinda as the hog of the wilderness tells us that this spirit is wild by nature and like the boar, amazingly sensitive to smells, sounds and changes in its environment, not to mention fierce. This is the power that helps you find plants in the wild and needs to be present when *macutos* (amulets), *bilongos* (magical medicines), and *mpolos* (magical powders) are made. He is also the power of the birds, especially nocturnal ones. The rarest birds like the nightjar announce his presence to the woods and to people. He is the protector of all things strange and unusual on the face of the earth and personifies the wild night. He is panic itself. He takes power at twilight and goes to rest at the break of dawn. He is the power that oversees the wild at night. He knows all its secrets and as the wild hog represents the essential nature of the wilderness. He is the most dense and untamed essence of all flora and fauna. No Palero can expect to be able to make his mumia work if his blessings are not attained as he is the one who sanctifies the collection of sticks and herbs so precious and necessary for creating the nkisi.

He is often syncretized with Osanyin/Osain, the Yoruba Lord of the Wild and in fact the vast corpus of material pertaining to the Cuban Osainistas or workers of his mystery do cross over and become virtually identical with the world of Gurunfinda. In the cult of Osain Eshu, Shango walks closely with Osain and this is also found in the importance of Nkuyu and Nsasi in the world of Gurunfinda. Nsasi is ever present in the *matari* or thunder stone in his mumia and Nkuyu by the blazing stars of animating ancestry that take flight in the nocturnal wilderness. When it comes to Gurunfinda the syncretism with Osain is quite perfect. Actually it almost seems like the Kongo infused the Yoruba Osain with much of their lore rather than the opposite way around. This is evident both in the ways an Osain is made in Cuba and also the material found in the various tratados used in his cult which can be quite easily applied to the cult of Gurunfinda.

To generate his mumia is a lengthy process as he needs exotic birds of various kinds, like the canary and parrot. He needs at least 101 sticks and shrubs, fungi and leaves to be present. He walks steadily with the help of turtle and toad and he flies on the wings of the parrot. Insects of various kinds are his allies and messengers and need to make part of his secret. He is the one nkisi that prefers vertebrae, finger and toe bones over the skull, as his voice and conscience is of the wilderness alone. Anything yet unborn and in the process of developing belong to him as holder of the necessary life force to bring a *mumia* into being.

Mambo for Gurunfinda:

> *Nganga Eh, Nganga mi lo*
> *Palo me lleva Pa'la Nfinda an Dio*
> *Ay Nganga Eh, Mi Nganga y Dio*
> *Palo me lleva Piako Piako ay Dio*
> *Nganga Eh, Nganga mi lo*
> *Zarabanda me lleva Pa'la Nfinda an Dio*
> *Nganga Eh, Nganga mi lo*
> *Siete Rayos me lleva Pa'la Nfinda an Dio*
> *Nganga Eh, Nganga mi lo*
> *Chola Wengue me lleva p ala Nfinda an Dio*
> *Nganga Eh, Nganga mi lo*
> *NN[§§] me lleva Pa'la Nfinda na Dio*
> *Nganga Eh, Nganga mi lo*
> *Centella Ndoki ca cuenda Nfinda an Dio*
> *Nganga Eh, Nganga mi lo*
> *Palo me lleva com su Magia an Dio*
> *Nzamiepungo me cutara Nsambia Dio*
> *Palo me lleva p ala Nfinda an Dio*

[§§] *Name of nfumbe*

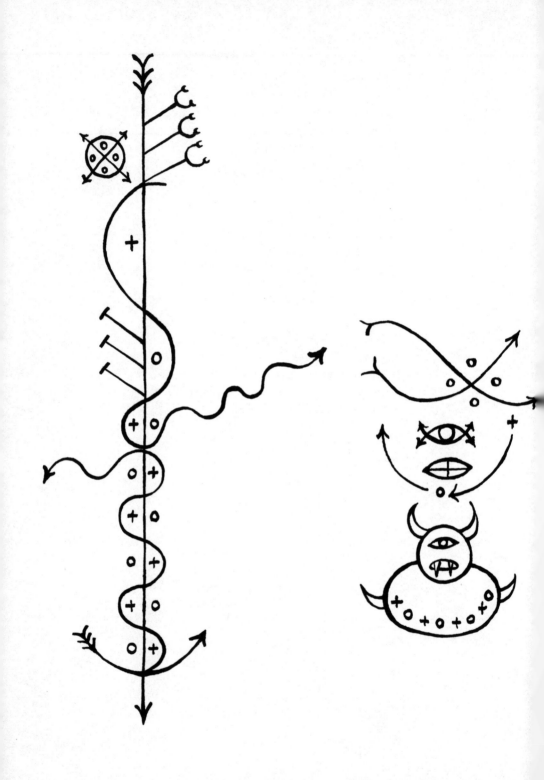

THE MYSTERIES OF LUKANKAZI

Lukankazi is an nkisi that has been syncretised with the Devil and in the same vein he is celebrated on Holy Friday, the day when Jesus Christ gave up his spirit and left a vacuum of power to be taken by his spiritual adversary. He is thus celebrated by placing his fundamento in a hole in the earth on burning coals in a ring of fire where his Tata then walks on fire and hot coals and manifests his presence. He was originally an mpungo of the sky and his name reveals an association with the heart of Nsazi, or the lightning. But like Pandilanga (Jesus Christ) he represents an anomaly that affirms the natural order. He is the most purging parts of the fire, its stillness associated with the blue flame closest to the wick of the candle. Since his fire is originally from Nsazi but animated in the material world it is conceived of as an antagonism. This is recounted in the record of one of his ceremonies by Natalia Bolivar Arostégui. She tells of a ceremony where you go to the cemetery on a moonless night and lighting a black candle in your left hand call Lukankazi by his name at the central cross and ask him to guide you to the proper tomb. Here you exhume the corpse and kill a black cat on it, this is the beginning of forming a pact. The cat will then be cut into pieces and buried at different locations in the cemetery and something taken from where the parts are buried. The head and slivers of the fur are kept in a vase filled with honey, bay laurel and all parts of the Ceiba. The corpse is then put back together with the vessel and it is all anointed with dry white wine. After seven days the corpse and the cat vessel is exhumed and the same procedure is repeated with a black dog. After another seven days, under the full moon, the body is again exhumed together with the cat and dog fetish. This time the skull and parts of hands, feet and ribs are taken along with the *luz* bone (sacrum) and the nganga is put together on the foundation of snake and thunderstone.

The idea is to unite antagonism, to make opposites work as one, but something else is also taking place. This mystery is demonstrated in the one eyed vampire firmas that belong to Lukankazi. His firmas are different from others and appear reminiscent of a cat like fiend with fangs and often one eye. At times similar firmas are given to Centella ndoki which speaks of a certain relationship between the powers of feline and bat that are united in her secret. Lukankazi is a nkisi originating from the rama called Tumba Franscesa, or Haitian Palo and the fundamento is ideally made from a Tata of this particular rama, thus we are speaking of a slightly different procedure than what is recounted here. The procedure told of here speaks of the essential nature of ndoki as being a state of ambivalence and conflict. Lukankazi is thus the principle of ndoki set on fire.

In Lukankazi we find the antagonistic story of Kongo meeting with the white predators that came sailing over the ancestral memory, the Kalunga and set fire to memory. Lukankazi as conflict and fire is also a principle of dramatic change and movement, a transformation that does not belong to the natural order. Lukankazi is starfire that burns over the earth, it is ambivalence which is naturally like cats and dogs, but in Lukankazi they have found a most dangerous unity. And herein is found the idea of ndoki as being something bad, as something that borrows its powers from the natural source of sorcery, Centella ndoki. From this line of thought it seems that the idea of sorcery in the Kongo mentality, both in its African and Creole reflections is related to setting the natural powers in motion, symbolized by the tornado, until the speed of motion leads to fire being ignited. Centella is considered cold, grave cold, but her powers can generate fire by moving the wind until friction – and thus fire – occurs. This tension is found in the icon of Lukankazi who over time took on the attributes of the Western devil. He represents the possibilities of the impossible, the fire that lurks threatening in the shadows of order.

Other names he is known by are Lucambe, Lungambe, Nkadiempemba, and Lukanzi.

An example of a work typically made at the feet of Lukankazi is one that finds a curious Western reference in the dreaded pactum diabolicum which in these cases often involves a pactum mortis, pacts with restless and vile dead ones upon taking 'the Devil' as your witness.

One example of malefica follows here:

You will at the feet of your prenda make a *chicherekú* (wooden doll representing both Nkuyu and the person you wish to harm). The greater the depth of trance the better the bilongo will work. You will then fill the image with ndokis which in this case is a reference to *weeds of the prenda*, i.e. matters rotten, dead and in decay.

You will then search out a proper nfumbe, meaning you will go to the cemetery and seek out the grave of a criminal or someone who died by his or her own hand. Here in a special ceremony you will make a pact with the nfumbe consisting of an exchange. You will take something from the grave and give the chicherekú in its place. This part is done without ceremony and the nfumbe will be enraged against the person represented by the chicherekú.

Mambo Lukankazi:

> *Lungambé no quiere a nadie*
> *Lungambé mato a su madre*
> *Lungambé mato a su padre*
> *Lungambé no tiene amigo*
> *Lungambé es gangulero*
> *Lungambé los Malos Palos*
> *Lungambé los Tronco Ceiba*
> *Lungambé los Tata Nfungue*

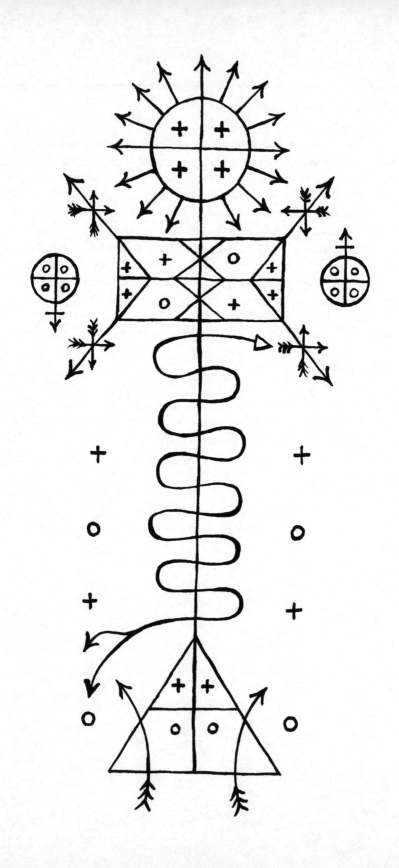

THE MYSTERY OF NGANGA KISSI

The Nganga Kissi also known as *Pandljaga* is responsible for divination and the mystery is most likely a metaphysical succession from the Kongo Ngoma cults, such as the Lemba and Nkita. The *ngombe* is a medium and the Ngoma cult or the Nganga ngoma was considered to be a seer and a soothsayer, a sage. Nowadays, ngoma simply signifies *medium* both in Cuba and Brazil and can be anyone, not necessarily a priest. This curiously enough replicates the way a nganga ngoma was elected in Kongo, namely by his qualities and mediumistic abilities. The nkisi itself is found in many prendas in what is called mpaka vititi, the *horn of the seer* or *seeing horn*. This replicates the idea of the classical Kongo wooden sculptures equipped with nails and a mirror placed over the secret contents in the region of the belly or the heart. Here the ancestors had a window out on the world and could by virtue of their double sight advise the living.

When it comes to the prenda itself there is a creative and interesting Cuban synthesis that reveals that the traditional Kongo perception of nkisi is very much intact. For some reason there are not sufficient representatives of the Ngoma cult to keep the tradition alive in the New World. Some of their teachings lived on in the horn of the seer and healing arts, but the cult itself seems distant in the larger scope of Palo Mayombe. This is curious, since the healing cult of the Ngoma was spread throughout what was called Kongo. Perhaps their importance was too great to be parted with from their native land? In Cuba the Ngoma cult was replaced with Ifá, a Yoruba cult that arrived in Cuba around 1850. The Nganga Kissi was then developed upon the mysteries of Ifá in the absence of Ngoma and replaced the spirit pot of the society of diviners or Kigoma. The Kissi is made from consecrated palm nuts, the ikins so sacred in Ifá and turned into the central secret within the nfumbe of the prenda. By doing this the nfumbe is animated with the spirit of Ifá and turns into Ngoma where its most essential feature is exactly that of the mpaka vititi. What actually happens is an abduction of a neighboring cult that is then reclothed in cultural values using a religious technology developed within their own cult in a way quite similar in nature to the Kongolese warrior societies.

This speaks of the warrior core of Palo Mayombe and displays for us the particular technology that is behind the gathering of the mumia and activation of the prenda. It speaks of Palo Mayombe as a traditional faith inspite of its creolization. Perhaps because of its rejection of conformity it managed to retain its traditional character and thus makes it possible to appraise the paleros as true spiritual warriors.

Ifa/Orunmila is syncretised in Kimbisa with St. Francis of Assisi and the mpungo in question is mpungo Lomboán Fula which means *the spirit who gives answers through the magical powders*. Lómbwa means *to wait for an oracular answer*, mfúla, later associated with fula or gunpowder is similar to mpólo, magic powder. The name indicates an active use of herbs and substances from nfinda, the wilderness, which ignite the oracular fire. Here we find a deep connection with Gurunfinda, Nkuyu and Mama Chola, who together with Cobayende generates the Yowa of contemporary Ngoma powers manifested in the Nganga Kissi.

Mambo for calling the inspiration of Nganga Kissi when throwing the oracle:

Glin, Glin, Glin, Chamalongo
Glin, Glin, Glin Chamalongo
Glin, Glin, Glin, Dame Alafia
Glin, Glin, Glin, Chamalongo

Glin, Glin, Glin, Aleja Okana
Glin, Glin, Glin, Chamalongo

Glin, Glin, Glin, Eyeife
Glin, Glin, Glin, Chamalongo

Glin, Glin, Glin, Son la hora
Glin, Glin, Glin, Chamalongo

Glin, Glin, Glin, Trae lo bueno
Glin, Glin, Glin, Chamalongo

Glin, Glin, Glin, Aleja malo

III NZO NTOTO

NZO NTOTO

THE TEMPLE OF LAND, STAR & EARTH

The idea of *nzo*, house/home, finds resonance both in the stars and in the *ntoto*, the earth, the land itself, which reflects the *ina* (light/fire) of Nzambi. The starry herd that follows Nkuyu does not deviate in essence from the starry bodies of the cosmos. The forest is the wilderness manifestation ntoto soaked in divine light, powers and inspiration. Everything that possesses virtue is nkisi, this invites us to take a sacred, albeit pragmatic, approach towards nature and the focus becomes how to find one's place in nature and establish one's centre, *nzo* – home. The palero is not only one of the *walking dead* he is also a spiritual warrior. He has conquered nature and established his nzo in the starlit ntoto. He has reinstalled the flame in corpses and unleashed his creative powers, manifesting Nzambi on earth.

The sacredness of nature is axial in Palo Mayombe and it uses the wisdom of the dead to guide the palero towards his own centre. I conceive of Palo Mayombe as pragmatic because of its focus on the creative potential in meeting with kimbiza, the powerful medicines of nature. It is about gaining insight into the natural law and understanding the powers residing in nature, be they visible or invisible. Palo Mayombe reflects a creative traditionalism. The traditionalism shines through in its *regla conga*, rules that are founded on a traditional world view. The creative element enters both through rama and the personal involvement that occurs at initiation. At times the rules are seen as dominant, as in any cult and religion that operates between the exoteric and 'esoteric'.

My own focus is of a more mystical and metaphysical character, I seek to embrace the creative spirituality at the heart of the cult. This perspective will at times be objected to by more exoteric focused paleros who delights in rules, hierarchy and dogmatic liturgical formats. I see the *regla* and the social controls that come with the cult as a good thing which guards the cult against improper individuals, but they do not necessarily have any significant bearing on the mystical dimensions of the practice itself.

The *rayamento*, literally cutting/scarring, in the initiation of a palero consists of a pact made with the nganga, but it is simultaneously a social responsibility in relation to ones rama. Rama, that is lineage, is crucial, as this is the fiery cord that connects the new palero with his ancestors and ancestry is what makes the palero a palero and not just a worker with dead bones. Given the nature of the cult I would dare say that any attempts to pull a nganga together moved by some perceived spirit contact, or because one sees this as merely a technology to be applied is both foolish and dangerous. Without the support of the rama the person making the nganga will generate offense and ridicule from true paleros, and is closing up the possibility of receiving future initiation. Also, the nature of the cult is such that without sufficient protection, which the rama constitutes, the bold and infantile manifestation of a nganga can turn into a devious nkisi that turns upon its maker and starts to feed on the vitality of its creator and his family. The rama are the long line of spirit guides which are particularly focused on guiding you as the new twig on the ancestral tree to wisdom and fullness. But more of this in the chapter *Jura!*

The palero works with the environment surrounding his nzo. This means that the task for someone outside Cuba who takes on the role of a palero should be to immediately start reorienting his nzo in conformity with the land where he lives. Guided by his nfumbe and Gurunfinda he will form a link with this specific environment and the spirits. The sorcerers that came from the Hills of Mayombe and Cabinda were met in the Diaspora with a nature that was both similar and different from that of their original homeland. They needed to enter into nature and understand the manifestations of the new land and its powers. This understanding can be absorbed by sharing knowledge with other practitioners, researching local folklore and in particular by the spiritual guidance arising from being connected to one's nfumbe.

All things in nature carry several levels of meaning, both directly and through their wider ecology or context. To develop an awareness or sensibility to this is the paleros challenge. It is through this route that he can gain the knowledge which brings an understanding of how to use and apply the spiritual gifts of nature.

In Palo Mayombe there are some plants, animals and natural phenomena that are more praised than others. This is similar to what we find in nature based faiths all over the world and in popular folk beliefs. The elephant is a symbol of strength and wisdom, the owl and raven bring bad omens but are also wise. The belladonna plant carries a sinister nightmare beneath her beauty, the oak is the king of the forest. Palo Mayombe is about being present in these natural realities and being inspired by them to develop a cunning craft. It is nature that gives us the advantage as we learn to turn the wheel of fate in conformity with its cycles. From this comes the idea of the palero as a sorcerer. Let us look at some ingredients in the arsenal of the typical Cuban palero to give an idea of what qualities are most sought after in the spirit haunted wilderness:

Arriero or the Great Lizard Cuckoo (*Saurothera merlini*) is a bird considered important because of its slyness and connection with the lunar cycles. Its presence is often seen as a bad omen as it warns of dishonorable behavior amidst ones closest kin. It is also seen as obsessive and its bones are sought after in works of binding. It is said that the binding by the bones of Arriero create a very violent obsession between those bound.

The Woodpecker (*Colaptes superciliaris*) is another bird considered important due to its dominion over trees. The trees are the source of the important palos, sticks freely give themselves to serve as platters for their food. Many paleros sees the woodpecker as the force that dominates the trees and as such represents the sum of domination over all palos.

Judio (*Crotophaga ani*), also known as Anu comes in many guises and is a relative of the cuckoo. Its name is given in reference to it being a manifestation of ndoki in the sense of the power that brings transformation and movement.

Kereketé (*Nyctibus griseus*) is another intriguing bird. In Europe it is known as the nightjar or hexen. It is valued for its relationship with the lunar cycles and prophetic abilities, but its appearance also makes it a suitable image for evil magical workings and the creation of nightmares.

Lechuza, which we know as the greater class of owls is important, both because the owl is the messenger of Mama Chola, but also because of its ability to inspire deep knowledge. It lends works of vengeance and violence a more devious and vile nature.

Loro, the Parrot, is another sacred and important bird, not only is it beautiful and blessed with a most stunning appearance, it can also speak. As such the parrot is both an omen of gossip as much as a symbol for the potency of accumulated wisdom.

Sabanero or *Piranga*, the Meadow Starling (*Sturnella ludoviciana*) is known in Chile as St. Peter and the bird is considered to be a wise bird with prophetic abilities.

Crocodile/Caiman (*Crocodylus rhombifer*) is for some the manifestation of Mama Chola, for others Nsasi. Popular belief says that the eggs are hatched only when thunder, lightning and storms are raging giving it an intense relationship with the creative principle as it is quickened by Nsasi. In nature it is patient, dangerous, sudden and inspires violence.

Somehow the palero needs to connect with these nkisi in order to use them. He needs to develop an understanding for what they are in themselves and in concert with other nkisi. The better grasp a palero has on nature, the better will his ngangas and bilongos work.

Herbs and palos that are frequently found in the paleros garden and munanso are given in the following little list. This list is by no means exhaustive, but rather is illustrative of the kinds of plants and the properties that are commonly found in the paleros natural arsenal.

Albahaca/Mecheiso also known as basil (*Ocimun basilicum*) is a wonderful herb with a multitude of good properties; it is good as a ward against the evil eye and it excites optimism and brings good fortune. As such it is a herb that is often used in despajos or cleansings.

Artemisa/Dioké (*Ambrosia artemisifolia*) is another great herb with powerful expelling qualities, but care must be taken as it is also a powerful abortifacient.

Carbonero/Naona (*Cassia biflora*) is another very useful plant. This shrub or small tree tends to divide itself in two, and has aphrodisiac qualities. It is reputed to stir sexual feelings and can be used in any situation that demands the manipulation of emotions. It is a wonderful shrub to use in works to reunite lovers and in all matters of a sexual and sensual nature.

Frescura (*Pilea microphyllia*) a brilliant green plant, relative of the cactus, this spreads fast and vigorously, it is often used for cleansings and as a remedy against restless and obsessive spirits.

Jiva Brava (*Casearia aculeata*). The plant is said to represent Lukankazi and holds strong antiseptic and anti-inflammatory properties. Recent research has also proven it to have some effect on autoimmune afflictions and conditions like chagas. Some paleros say the plant represent Lukankazi when he demands respect.

Jiqui/Ntuenke (*Pera bumelifolia*) the heart of this plant serves for the mati mati of the nganga and cuts any witchcraft. It is seen as being proud, solid, alert and very defensive. It creates stability.

Jucaro Bravo (*Bucida buceras*) or the Black Olive Tree, also simply called *the Nail*, is a tree with magnificent properties. It is a great expeller and dominator. It is also good to use in works of control and to both ease and create chaos. It is particularly good in cases where the law is involved.

Cereke/Laurel (*Ficus nitida*) is a well known plant, which in Palo is used to inspire confidence, loyalty and protection. Many paleros consider it essential for making any nganga given its admirable qualities.

Lechero (*Sapiumi jamaicensis*) a sub species of the already large genus euphorbiaceae that possess excellent exorcising properties

Yaba (*Andira jamaicensis*) is a distant relative of the almond and is also known as bastard almond. It is sacred to Lukankazi, and as with all of his plants carries both vermifuge properties and is to some extent narcotic. The Yaba is particularly toxic and is said to bring blindness and insanity to enemies. Considered extremely malefic and poisonous it is at times also taken as the Palo Diavolo.

THE WORLD OF BILONGO

Bilongo is medicine of any kind and takes the form of powders, baths and workings done for the prenda or under the influence of the prenda. We must remember that whatever the palero does the prenda always follows.

Purifications and baths make up an important part of Palo Mayombe and should be considered integral to the work of the practitioner. Given the intimate congress with dense and at times hostile spiritual influences it is of great importance to maintain the soul in an elevated state. Some paleros describe these hostile and malevolent influences as being naturally attached to the palero because he is an anomaly. He is the walking dead carrying a forceful light. He is light embodied in the sensual world and as such has become something other, a memory that attracts all kinds of spirits, no matter what their intent.

The bath of the palero is given several names, but frequently it is called by the lukumi term *omiero*. Omiero is from the yoruba *omi*, water, and *èrò* denoting something macerated or marshy. It is a water of power and is the magical bath or lustral waters of the palero. These baths can serve a great variety of purposes. The baths are usually made by macerating leaves that are prayed and sung over to charge them, in order to turn the herbs and waters into a water of power. It is also quite common to add to the finished bath a piece of burning coal, *fioteke*, representing Nsasi and Vence Bataya. When making baths the gathering of herbs is always done under the influence of Seke or Gurunfinda. Ideally you enter nfinda in the hour before the sun is rising and gather herbs still wet with the dew of the night. When the herbs are macerated it is good to pray and sing to the nkisi you make the bath in respect of. It is always good to use a mambo to generate the contact and upon being touched by spirit I find it quite helpful to allow the heart to take over the words and move the mambo and prayers. Some formulas are given here to present an idea of how the palero works with some of the most useful magical baths.

· *A cleansing for the house to bring peace and tenderness by using Baluande* ·

Make the firma of Lucero Quatro Vientos and heat a piece of coal which you place in a small earthenware jar which is then placed on the firma with a lemon. Cut the lemon into four pieces and place a pinch of sea salt on each quarter. Place them at the four corners of the house.

Then take leaves of melon, the petals and leaves of marigold, the petals of blue lotus and flowers and/or leaves of cherry. Macerate these plants with one part aguardiente, one part dry white wine, one part coconut water and seven parts of water. Sing to Baluande and keep the purpose of the bath firmly in mind. Into the bath charged by this vinculum you will drop the hot coal, then remove the leaves from the water and place them upon the firma of Lucero. These leaves you will later burn and turn into mpolo which will carry these same qualities. Then take the water in a bucket and let if slowly flow over you from the head down. Take this bucket and use its omiero to wash the house with a happy heart and pray at all times to Baluande. You will start from the front door of the house and end at the back door. When all the floors and in particular all the corners have been purified, leave the bucket outside the back door until the next morning. Gather the pieces of lemon and put them in the water and take the water to a crossroads away from the house and throw the water and lemon there.

· *A bath for tranquility with Tiembla Tierra* ·

A wonderful bath for bringing calmness to the mind and dispelling negativity is this bath made under the influence of the earth shaker Tiembla Tierra. This bath is also good to use when you are confronted with difficult choices. The procedure is similar to the above bath. In this bath you will combine Tingoro *(Jathropa diversifolia)*, Palo Amarillo *(Cocconia frutescens)*, coconut water, a cup of goat's milk and some patchouli. Draw the firma of Tiembla Tierra in front of Lucero and place the bucket on top of it. Place four white candles around the bucket. Macerate the plants in the liquids while you pray and sing asking to dispel the negativity. This being done drop the burning coal and remove the herbs and let them dry together with the coal and turn them into ashes that you will then use for making a mpolo. Every morning for three days consume these ashes mixed with goat's milk and honey.

· *A war bath made under the aegis of Zarabanda* ·

Take Palo Amargo *(Picramnia reticulate)*, Palo Blanco *(Simarouba glauca)*, Palo Vencedor *(Zanthoxylum arboreum)* and make from them an mpolo. Then take dried leaves of Guava, leaves of chilli peppers, cayenne peppers and three pods of alligator peppers. Gather this in a vessel and present it to Lucero Malongo or on the firma of Lucero Cuatro Vientos in front of Zarabanda. Light two candles, one white and one black and feed Zarabanda with *chamba* (a sacred fiery drink) and *fula* (gunpowder) placed on the firma in such way that the target is marked. You will then take the powders and leaves and place them into a basin with two parts strong alcohol and 8 parts water and bring it up to heat. The bath should be taken when it is a bit too hot. This being done you will go to Zarabanda with one cup of this water and feed it to him with chamba and a rooster or quail and start your nocturnal bilongos.

· Some mpolos ·

Mpolos or powders can be made from anything in nature, be it animal, vegetable or mineral. The mpolos are always made in the presence of your prenda and the items you intend to use are presented to nfumbe and/or Gurunfinda, as license to use them must be sought and granted. Some of these mpolos are very simple and effective. They can be added to the target's food after being charged. One such simple and effective mpolo is to turn Palo Peralejo (*Brysonima crassifolia*) into a powder while singing to Mama Chola, constantly declaring your purpose. This powder is used to make a man lose his virility, either in terms of lust or potency. Another one which serves well when you seek to alter someone's opinion or change their mind is to work Palo Cuaba/ Palo Cambia (*Amyris balsamifera*) into a powder under the influence of Nkuyu. If you seek to sweeten someone take Palo Dominador, Palo Ramon (see PART IV), hibiscus flowers, petals of roses and orchids and present them first to Lucero. If possible let the petals and leaves dry in front of him. You will then at the feet of Baluande turn this into a most potent mpolo.

· Bilongos for various ends ·

To *create great disturbance with Cobayende* you will take mustard seeds, sesame seeds, chili peppers, peanuts, cat feces and dog feces and turn this into a mpolo at the feet of Cobayende on his war firma. You will then add the firma to the powder and blow it on the land or the house of the person you seek to disturb. This is an interesting mpolo as it actively uses one of the taboos of Palo Mayombe, namely sesame seeds. Sesame seeds agitate the dead in very negative ways and must never be used as a part of the prenda or in bilongos to gain favors. Some paleros says that the best way of dismantle a prenda is to fill it with sesame seeds and bury it inside an anthill. This speaks volumes about the nature of sesame seeds.

To *create havoc and turmoil with Vence Bataya* you will take the name of the person written on a piece of red cloth. You will spray the name with chamba, and place a pinch of nfumbe powder and a pinch of pepper seeds on it and fold it into a square. Then take Mansagro (*Macfadyena unguis cacti*) Malacara (*Plumbago scandens*) and Camaguey (*Stigmaphyllon sagreanum*) and tie them in the red cloth where the name of the person you seek to hurt is written. Sacrifice a quail on the bundle and leave it with Vence Bataya or Lucero for three nights, burning candles constantly. Then take the bundle and bury it at the gate of the house of the one you seek to harm.

•

To *make guardians of the house with Zarabanda* you will take mpolo Palo Diavolo (see PART IV), mpolo nfumbe, mercury, peppers, beeswax, a train track nail, fula, ntoto from the police station and four crossroads that carry the vibration of protection and force, and some red ribbons. Bring this to Zarabanda and call your nfumbe and ask him to empower your offering. Mix the ingredients with the beeswax and apply them to the nail, wrap it in ribbons and place it on the firma of Zarabanda or Lucero. Offer a rooster and let it rest until the next night when you bury it at the gate of your house. Better still is if you make two nails, one to guard the front door and one to guard the back door.

•

To *win a court case with Tiembla Tierra or Zarabanda* you take bark of cinnamon, Palo Raspalengua (*Casearia hirsute*), hibiscus, cascarilla, quicksilver, mpolo of pheasant feathers and on a piece of white cloth write the name of the judge and your own name crossed. Anoint it with honey, fold it and seal it with beeswax. Gather the other items on another white cloth and place the names inside it. Offer a pigeon and let it rest until the night after when you wrap it up in white cord and carry it with you as a macuto. When the case is done give the macuto to your prenda and offer a rooster.

To *open opportunities with* Lucero you will write your name seven times on the leaves of Abre Caminho and present them on the firma of Lucero, add to this mpolo of Palo Jaguey (*Ficus trigonata*), valerian root and seeds and petals of sunflower. Let it dry at the foot of Lucero for three days and wrap it in a red cloth and seal it with cowry and beeswax. Give a quail to the macuto.

·

To *break off negativity with* Tiembla Tierra *and* Centella you will take ginger root, Mastuerzo (*Scoparia dulcis*), four sticks of Palo Ramon (see PART IV), cloves, feather of Mayimbe and Orange flowers. You will gather these items on a black cloth and place it on the firma of Lucero Quatro Vientos and light four white candles at the corners. Call Lucero and Tiembla Tierra or Centella and take a pinch of the ntoto from their prenda and add it to the contents on the cloth. Let it rest on the firma until the next night. Wrap it up and gather it between the palos, tie it up with white cord or leather and place it on Centella or Tiembla Tierra and offer a chicken. Let it rest until the next night and take the bundle and present it to the four corners of your home before burying it in front of the munanso.

·

To *attract someone with* Mama Chola you will take Lechera (*Euphorbia heterophylla*), Vergonzosa (*Mimosa pudica*), convolvulus/poppy, Palo Dominador (see PART IV), roses, brown sugar and sandalwood. Take a knife and write the name of the person you seek to attract on the palo. Write your own name five times on a piece of paper and burn it in front of Mama Chola (or on her firma in front of Lucero) and add it to the ingredients. Gather this inside a red cloth and tie it to the palo. Give it a pigeon and let it rest on Mama Chola or with Lucero.

To *bring negativity to someone's life with* Centella or Mama Chola you will write the name of the person on a piece of dirty cloth, or a cloth that has been used to wash your house for a long time. Place this inside the husk of a coconut and add to this rock salt, sulfur, graveyard dirt, feces of rat, bat or cat, mpolo Palo Rompe Zaraguey (*Eupatorium odoratum*) preferably its root, rat-weed (*Psychotria tabacifolia*) mpolo nfumbe, mpolo of the shell of a turtle. Cover this with ntoto ndoki and add a drop of mercury. Seal the husk and place it with Centella for the night whilst burning black candles. The night after take it to the house of the one you seek to harm and bury it at his gate.

VITITI

THE ART OF SEEING

The word *vititi* is from the kikongo *mbititi*, which means *sight*, *to see* and *look into*. The oracle most often employed for vititi is the use of *chamalongos*. The chamalongos are most commonly made up from the hard shell of the coconut, the concave or inside being its speaking side and its outer husk the non-speaking side. Chamalongo is from the kikongo *kiamalongo*, which means *little treatise*. The Capuchin missionaries used this word in reference to the catechism and smaller sermons. It referred to how divine messages were conveyed and this fits quite well with the nature of how the chamalongos work. They serve as a means for communication with spirit.

The chamalongos can be used to answers questions in a simple yes/no fashion. As the relationship with the nfumbe develops so also does the oracle and it turns into a means for fuller communication, a vinculum of union itself. A palero with a strong bond with his prenda will use the chamalongos as a tool for communication that goes beyond its simple binary response. As the oracle falls, a certain inspiration or understanding is also given which gifts the palero with a most productive and revealing vinculum with his nfumbe in the form of a spiritual discourse.

Two of the most frequently employed oracles in Palo Mayombe are the chamalongos and the Vititi Nkobos, or *seeing shells*. The chamalongos are four pieces of coconut (some use five, but the fifth is not thrown, serving instead as a witness in the guise of Nkuyu). Some also use the larger brown cowry shells for this purpose. The chamalongos follow the same idea contained in the Yowa cosmogram and thus creation. It also reflects the mystery of Angoro and Angoromea (also known as *nzimba*, the sacred twins). It is here we find the circles o manifested in the untold possibility, the backside or the silent mouth representing ntoto, earth. The use of **+** represents Nzambi's positive manifestation and the speaking mouth.

The procedure is simple; the chamalongos are tapped on the prenda three times and then on the ground three times while a prayer is recited. The way the parts fall reveals the answer. The messages of the marks are as follows:

++++ *Four parts speaking:*
Matuba speaks of good fortune being manifested.

+++o *Three parts speaking:*
Kisalu speaks of good fortune coming by applying correct focus and indicates some struggle towards the goal.

++oo *Two parts speaking:*
Budelele speaks of good fortune coming by the balancing of good and bad. It is a most auspicious mark.

+ooo *One part speaking:*
Nzanza speaks of the spirit of uprising, rebellion and conflict.

oooo *All parts closed:*
Kufwa speaks of death, obscurity and night, the end of a cycle.

In addition there are also some other configurations that are worthy to note. If the chamalongos fall in a straight line, this is a good omen. If one chamalongo parts from the others and jumps towards the prenda, the solution lies with the prenda. Two chamalongos falling with the silent side up close to the prenda warns against false accusations, betrayal and problems with the police surfacing. The speaking side signifies the presence of females and the silent side signifies the presence of males. Nzambi's positive presence in the world is in a mysterious way always female.

Call to start the session from the Changani rama:

Aguiri Nkuto guiri ndinga mapangui enbua de nchila mati
Com Licencia to lo nfumbe
Que cuenda munanso kongo ingenio la asuncion
Licencia Lucero
Licencia Nganga
Bendicion Padrino Kuenda

Alternatively there is this call from the Nkita rama, which is found in many varieties in other ramas. This can also be used to instigate bilongo:

Nkita kinseke mundo
Nkita kinseke yaya
Espíritus del mundo!
Espíritus fuertes!
Vamo a labora
Vamos a trabajar
Nkita kinseke yaya
Espíritus fuertes!
Vamo a laborá!
Vamos a trabajar
El palo yaya vamos a trabajar
El palo tengui vamos a trabajar
El palo brujo vamos a trabajar
Kuni kano vamos a trabajar
La Ceiba vamos a trabajar
Nfumbi bueno! Muerto bueno!
Arriba na mundo!

VITITI NKOBO

THE NINE ORACULAR SHELLS OF THE NGOMBE

Before the shells are prepared, the closed part of the cowry is broken and washed in a specially prepared lustral water. The selection of herbs and mpolos is in conformity with the teachings of the individual rama.

After washing the shells and charging them a lifeforce offering is given, which is usually two white pigeons, together with shea butter, coconut, cascarilla (white chalk) and perfumes. The vessel is then covered with a white cloth for three days and on the fourth day it is washed again with river water and filled with the secret mpolo that turns the cowry into the *vititi nkobo*, or the seeing shells. The nkobos speak according to their marks. A mark designates a particular pattern made from the speaking and closed parts of the nkobo. The speaking part is the natural opening of the shell. Each mpungo/nkisi has their mark or marks. The shells are thrown twice. The first throw determines if the message is positive or negative. If the number of speaking shells in the first throw is greater than in the second throw the nkobos give good news, if it is the other way around, the interpretation of the mark is as a negative oracle. The nkobos are thrown twice, but there are three marks that do not require a second throw as they convey a unique message of both good and ill – but are read in a positive light. These are the mark of Tiembla Tierra (sign number 8); Zarabanda (sign number 3); Cobayende (sign number 10). It is also possible to use the chamalongos to define if the marks fall in a positive or negative way or you can simply take four nkobos and throw them in the fashion of the chamalongos.

The reading of the nkobos is done in similar fashion to the chamalongos with the difference being the complexity of the message revealed by the nkobos. As with the chamalongos, the pattern formed is also taken into consideration and not simply how many mouths are speaking. If one nkobo falls at the feet of the diviner it is a sign that the nkisi is in disagreement with the session itself and an investigation of the cause must be made. If two nkobos fall mouth up it denotes friendship amongst two women. A gathering of three or more nkobos in a cluster speaks of a good bond between as many men as are gathered around the shells. If a nkobo that has fallen with its mouth open and one or two nkobos falls with its mouth over it, it reveals that a woman has a lover, and perhaps more than one. If the nkobo falls with its mouth to the ground and one or two shells with the mouth upon its back, it means that the man has a lover or more. A nkobo on top of another can indicate foolishness on the part of a woman. The mouth down on another mouth can be indicative of struggles, often a sign of someone seeking to defeat the client. Three nkobos mouth up with some mounted on top of them speaks of lewdness amongst women. If the nkobos are inverted, i.e. mouth down, with others clustering on top it is a sign of lewdness among men, or weakness of character. If in a throw a nkobo falls alone in the centre it usually represents alienating situations, losing friends or that he is being persecuted by the law. It is customary to embark on a new reading if such a mark appears. A nkobo falling mouth down and two falling to its side with the mouth open represents a man who is dominated by two women; if it falls with one mouth up with two more to each side mouth down it indicates that the woman is dominated by two men. If all the nkobos fall with the mouth up over those mouth down it augurs good. In the same manner the reverse gives bad omens. A mouth that speaks is fortunate, and it speaks of misfortune when the mouth falls to the ground.

THE MARKS OF THE NKOBOS

1 · Yosi (9 shells that don't speak)

This is a bad mark and is not read. In this case the ngombe will gather all the nkobos in a jar of water and pray over it. The nkobos are removed and the water thrown outside on the street. Three crosses are marked on the door of the munanso with cascarilla and a line is stretched across the floor from the last cross. This can also be done with shea butter or cacao butter. Rub the nkobos with a bit of the butter and blow on them three times praying that they speak well. Place them back in the cup and pray over them. Then take four of the nkobos and ask your prenda if you have license to read for the person in front of you. If the answer is yes, continue the reading after giving something to your prenda. If the answer is no, a negative influence is indeed revealed. In this case the nkobo are again placed in a cup of water but this time you need to add perfume, rum, three pinches of tobacco and a piece of cacao butter. The nkobos are removed and the mixture is thrown on the ground, not the street, whilst praying that the malefica the person brought will go away. This mark reveals the presence of nkisi ndoki who are out searching for human blood. You need to ask permission of Nsambi and Nsasi to re-move all evil influences and bad bilongo done to the person. A trap has been set for the client and he needs to open his eyes, and be mindful of hidden enemies. A proverb says: *There is no worse goad than the same stick.* This mark speaks of someone close to the client who is secretly work-ing against him using bad bilongo. It speaks of the fatal consequences of the evil eye and of greed being directed towards the client. A bath must be prepared with seven herbs that stimulate the warrior within. Clean the person with a white plate, and then place a white candle in its centre. The person is then turned seven times to the left and seven times to the right. He must then be cleansed with two white pigeons which must be released and not sacrificed. A rooster is then taken and the client is cleansed with it. His clothes must be removed and given to the prenda while the cleaning with the animal happens and the white plate must be broken at the end of the cleansing. The clothes are then returned, the broken plate is placed on the prenda and the animal is given. The client will then take the broken plate together with a bottle of aguardiente and a cigar and leave this in the cemetery.

2 • *Yole* (*1 mouth speaking*)

This mark is said to speak of the presence of Nzimba, the sacred twins, but it is also a mark where Zarabanda and Nkuyu (Lucero) speaks. It is crucial to pay attention to Lucero. Nkuyu malongo is the one who dominates the client's life. It speaks of two spirits joined together which were born dead and Lucero Malongo who has two faces, one in the front and one in the back. It speaks about confrontations with justice, about general legal problems and losing arguments and discussions. It speaks of slanderous rumors and trickery. You have to be careful about whose company you keep. The client must be cleansed with fire. If the orientation is positive it signals a favorable outcome; he is going to win in legal problems, will recognize his enemy and will triumph in the end over all tribulations. There is also likely to be a change of, or improvement at work, possibly a raise or promotion. Take care of the eyes. You will know the causes of your past, present and future misfortunes. You will receive a blessing and those who are envious will try to prevent it, but will not accomplish this. You are clearheaded, but sometimes you are lacking initiative. Do not swear or use bad words. Ask if the client needs to be scratched (scarred) or if there is any spiritual obligation that will open his road. A head cleansing is good. If the orientation is negative it speaks of all things bad and how the client will go from bad to worse. You used to remember your dreams and visions. They are blocked now. You do not realize that evil has crossed you. At times this sign is an indication that receiving a prenda will open their path. Getting a prenda under this mark ensures faithful guidance from the dead. Be careful of deceitful paleros. Give blessings and prayers to Nkuyu. You must give to Nkuyu a rat, or at least its head. For the head cleansing you can use smoked fish, two roosters, *jutía* (rat), coconut, cacao butter or shea butter, toasted corn, honey, aguardiente and water. Lucero Malongo speaks in this mark reminding you that all things have two faces. Give to the munanso a bottle of brandy, a bundle of candles, black and red cloth and an additional fee. Take a bath with herbs of Tiembla Tierra.

3 · Itatu (2 mouths speaking)

Zarabanda speaks and says you do not need to look to the right or the left. There is no need to throw a second time. Zarabanda speaks directly. This person has trouble with the law; a deadly fight or tragedy, aside from a spiritual challenge, where a nfumbe or mpungo is drawn to the person. It is both good and bad. Lucero also speaks as well as

Chola Wanga and the nfumbe. You've had problems at work and must exercise caution to not lose your job. Someone who is incompetent at work envies you. To protect against this misfortune, prepare a bilongo at the foot of Zarabanda. Use dirt of the caldron, dirt from your shoes, from your work, smoked fish, dried rat, a coin, and lodge this in corn-meal. Place this inside a piece of bamboo and seal it with beeswax. Feed it to two quails and leave it with Zarabanda in order to avoid problems, confusion and disagreements. Don't use or carry weapons of any kind and do not keep them in your house as this will draw hostility to you. Do not discuss anything illegal with anybody at all nor do anything illegal. Someone will try to destroy a relationship between a man and a woman and there will be an attempt to destroy the peace in your home through wickedness, infidelity and bilongo. There is a need to commit to a religious discipline or a religion, this will give great protection. Clean the client with a black rooster, two coconuts, two white candles, dry white wine or cognac. Trace in front of the nganga a triple line with the mbele and with the Tata and the client standing on the lines, give the bilongo to the client. A positive orientation speaks of a good spirit coming forth, of African origin that will help him as a palero. This is the spirit of an old palero. Since he has not committed himself to the cultivation of the spirits of the prenda, this helpful spirit is being experienced as intrusive and troublesome. This mark warns you that although you can experience a tragedy or risk imprisonment, the tragedy will be without great consequence and you will be released from prison. Stability in the workplace and in your business is likely as long as you are well prepared and are friendly. It is recommended that you to have a *limpieza* (cleansing) and three or seven baths (divination is necessary to see what herbs are needed). A head cleansing to Nsasi is recommended and also to receive nkisi Zarabanda. Guard the door to your house with a guardian nkisi. Do not stop in crossroads or corners nor meet with anyone at these places. For some time avoid visiting people in their home because they may ask favors of you that you will find difficulties complying with and this can generate enmity. Never lose your temper with anybody, because it can have bad consequences for you. Avoid alcoholic drinks. Be careful of any accident involving the legs or feet because you may suffer a long time, you may even lose them. Avoid attracting the attention of the police or it will bring trouble to your family. It will be beneficial to surrender to Zarabanda. It might also be necessary to make a *nsala* (a defensive working) with the tongue of an ox or a *nkanda* (binding) using the tongue of a bird – all at the feet of Zarabanda. Wear white as much as possible and get a medallion of Zarabanda (San Pedro/San Miguel) to keep under your shirt. Clean your house with herbs and cleanse the door. If this reading verifies a negative presence the client should go straight to the feet of Zarabanda. Someone will come to you offering a business deal or a job. Think long and hard before accepting it. Avoid married women because you will abandon your house as a result of such a relationship. Her triumph will be your disgrace. If you see someone running, don't follow them, avoid them. You need to make a cleansing with one rooster which will be sacrificed, and one quail for the head cleansing (rogacion), two white pigeons that will be released, two fresh fish, cacao or shea butter, smoked fish, toasted corn, coconut, rat, aguardiente, a bundle of candles, a bottle of dry white wine, cognac, cigars, a new chain and a knife and an additional fee.

4 · Iya (3 mouths speaking)

Nsasi, Nsimba (the twins) Mama Chola and Lucero Quatro Vientos speak in this mark. It speaks of a union of these four forces. If the shells fall towards the centre Tiembla Tierra is entering the design and must be consulted. The mark speaks of something good coming your way. It is necessary to investigate what important actions the client has left undone, what promises are left unfulfilled. For some reason Nsasi is blocking the opportunities of this person. This mark tells that the client is going through a very bad situation which is caused by the involvement of another. This bad condition is not of the person's sole making, but instigated by someone else. If it is a woman that is being read for, this mark tells that her man treats her very badly. He has become bored with her and treats her as a slave. Attend to your house, and attend to your husband. Avoid provoking abortions of any kind, whether by herbs, a doctor's hand, or ill will and resentment directed towards the foetus. If it is a man this reading says that you have a female enemy who is working bilongo against you, most likely by purchasing services from someone else. This woman's goal is to imprison him. Nsasi says to be careful, because a serious offense is about to be committed. Avoid the company of people who use drugs or are criminals. You had a dream which you have not yet been able to turn into reality because of your lack of faith. You are destined to be rich. For cleansing use a rooster, four pigeons, one candle and two coconuts. Even if the mark is positive you need to be careful. Don't keep bad company and be patient. Wait for the promise Mama Chola made you. You need to do the cleansing you were told to before the nganga. If the mark answers in the negative, do not let yourself be carried away by your impulses. Such behavior will send you to prison. You have a woman who tricks you with tears. Do not use drugs for it will be your demise. Protect your genitals and do not be promiscuous, don't sleep around and don't say too much. It is recommended you get a good macuto as part of your limpieza.

5 · Itanu (4 mouths speaking)

Mama Chola and Centella speak in this mark. If the consultant is a man, he has problems with a woman. A separation has been discussed. The situation has been caused by the man finding himself in a conflict between two women. You have stomach problems which are caused by bilongos one of your women has made. Beware of impotency and pay attention to your daughter(s). Centella says you are surrounded by enemies and advises you to change your environment. It would be good to move. Change the position of the furniture in your house. You are viewed as a difficult person and no matter how you give or take you find yourself unable to please people. You need to change your style of speech, because even if you are content, it appears that you are bothered and it will hurt your attempts to communicate. Your house needs a *despojo* (cleansing). Prepare a candle with corn meal, place the candle in a pumpkin filled with honey and light the wick. On the positive side of this mark Mama Chola says that the separation you have experienced was due to an abusive person. Do not raise your hand towards an elder or a woman, no matter what. Don't be ill mannered, nor refuse a hand which offers to help, don't offend anyone. You need to take a bath with parsley, cinnamon, calming herbs, cornmeal, and honey in order to expel the ill will of Mama Chola. You must move if you want to avoid death. On the negative or left side Centella speaks and says that even though an enemy will destroy him, he must return what he took or be alone. Apart from the candle which you must burn, you must make a bath with herbs of Mama Chola and Baluande mixed with honey, rum, tobacco and perfume.

6 · Sabami (5 mouths speaking)

In this mark speaks Nsasi and Lucero Quatro Vientos. In this mark you should pay attention to both the bad and good parts of the message. Centella Ndoki is also present in this mark. It is necessary in this mark to divine if the throw is negative for the client or the palero. This being done Nsasi will speak directly. You are broke or low on resources, you should place something red in a prominent location in your house. Be careful with your business, it might get easily troubled. Don't lie to your partner or you will lose their trust. Be very careful with the law. Collect 12 *quimbombo* (stones) at a crossroads and gather them behind your door. You need to visit a babalawo. If the throw is positive Nsasi speaks on behalf of Centella that grudges and envy abides. Someone desires to give you good things, but with your delinquent behavior you are pushing this away. You need to get serious with your life and prepare for good things in a serious way. Build confidence and don't lose courage. If the mark falls in the negative there is a danger of being assaulted, your attitude brings this to you. To avoid this you must cense yourself with garlic powder and throw brown sugar on the incense. Purify the workplace with powerful purgatives and cleansing herbs and place garlic above the door of your business. You must hang 12 chilli peppers at the top of the door. You need to get a Lucero.

7 · *Sabuadi (6 mouths speaking)*

Baluande and Maniquilla speak in this mark and declare that your wealth is to be found in the countryside. You need to cross the ocean and find your fortune in foreign lands. If you haven't done so yet, you will. It is not good for you to live a predictable life, you need movement. Visit with great frequency woods and mountains. Venerate the old and ancestral. Delve into the waves of the sea and make requests to her. Do whatever Baluande asks of you and always settle your scores and debts, because in this life nothing is ever free. Analyze the successes and failures of your business. Observes well, the changes of the moon and how they are reflected in your character, in your health and mood. You owe a promise to Baluande. Have you dreamt of a woman dressed in blue? Clean your house with several herbs but select them with care, do not use just any herb. Play a game of chance, but do not tell anyone, keep it a secret. If the mark falls out favorably Baluande says the trip you are planning will be a success. You will receive money through a game of chance. You need to change your character as you have two personalities. You need to take a bath in the sea and leave the sea backwards, ask the ocean to help you change your attitude and to guide you. If it falls negatively it is important that you honor your promises and you need to have made a collar with 7 segments of different colours and wear it for 7 days. You will then give it to the waves of the sea and let her take it away. There is also advice from Maniquilla that you need to take care of your health. In this mark the hole was first dug and water flowed in – be careful that you don't drown, both in the ocean itself or in emotions. You must clean your house with lavender, grape leaves, dry white wine, aguardiente and herbs of Baluande.

8 · *Nana (7 mouths speaking)*

Mama Kengue/Tiembla Tierra speaks and you do not need to throw a second time. You might use the four nkobos to determine if it falls in a positive or negative way. The client, if it is man or woman is unhappy in love and has many vices. Be careful with alcohol, drugs or marijuana. This person is musical and creative. Under this mark all nfumbe are coming to your aid and seek to protect and commune with you. Because of this you may be victorious in all that is possible and impossible. Although you have many enemies you may triumph over them. At times sadness may overcome you. You feel bad for those less fortunate and you are greatly affected by the death of those whom you know or of family members. You should avoid frequenting cemeteries, hospitals and especially prisons. You should seek to get a prenda of nfumbe. Do not be jealous. If the person is white a black woman may fall in love with them and vise versa. You will soon embark on a journey. This will be important for you. Get an interpretation of your dreams and visions, there is much here you are missing. You should take a bath with fresh herbs of Tiembla Tierra and add to this cascarilla and milk. Dress in white as often as possible. If the person is a woman she should refresh her head with green coconut milk and cascarilla. Avoid harming people and do not harbor grudges and do not curse. Adore the sun and have a cleansing done at the feet of Quatro Vientos. Make a bath of cotton seeds, cascarilla, dry white wine, egg whites, rainwater and orange blossom water. Pray on this upon the firma of Quatro Vientos.

If it falls positively it advises you to remain serious about your talents and develop your creative abilities, especially for music. You are a child of the saints, so do not argue, don't be jealous of anything or anybody. Make frequent baths with fresh herbs and respect the words of your elders. If it falls in the negative be careful with your vices. Avoid visiting cemeteries, jails and hospitals. You should bathe with herbs of Tiembla Tierra together with rainwater, orange blossom water, seawater, swamp water and aguardiente.

9 · Fua (8 mouths speaking)

This is the mark of Mariwanga but Cobayende follows this sign as a shadow. This is a mark of bad luck, infirmity and failure to carry out ones promises. It speaks of the dead, about theft and insolence of all kinds. Centella Ndoki speaks directly here and demands your word to be given and your promise to be kept. Do not wear clothes that are not your own and do not wear torn or holed clothes. You have a scar on your body. Be careful because the dead walk in your house. Someone whom you care for is going to change. Avoid being out in the streets at midnight. Be careful of Mariwanga and do not play with her. Bilongos directed at others may turn toward you. If the mark falls in the positive the person has to wear his or her shirt inside out for a day. Never be the third person in a group. In this mark it is common to suffer fatigue and headaches. This mark also speaks of excess of acidity. If it is a woman, her period is irregular; she should go to the doctor to have it checked. Be careful with cooking fires and of bilongo thrown in your food. Avoid foul language. You need to bathe in herbs of Mama Chola and *rompe zaraguey* mixed with blessed water. You also need to take some of the cologne/perfume the person is using and a bit of ash from fumigations to clean the person. If it falls in the negative it speaks of a person who is already haunted by many problems and financial difficulties. Their health is in decay. If it is a man it speaks of problems with the prostate and this mark also speaks of problems with the kidneys, blood pressure and cholesterol. Generous amounts of water should be consumed and a medical check up done urgently. They are an easy target for bilongo ndoki. To avoid this prepare a candle in the husk of a coconut in a mixture of rum and oil and place in this a cotton wick. Place this afloat in a larger dish filled with water and light it.

10 · Kumi (9 mouths speaking)

This is the mark of Cobayende. When it appears throw three drops of water on the ground. Then mark the forehead, throat and the nape of the neck of the querant with water. In this mark also speaks Mariwanga and Mama Chola. Refresh the nkobos with water and throw the water on the doorstep and empty all vessels of uncovered water that are in the house. Once this is done, collect the nkobos and throw them again. If the same sign falls again then it indicates that Mariwanga, Centella

Ndoki and Mama Chola are speaking. They speak of women's battle, curses and bilongo. Take the Nkobo and cleanse them with perfume, rum, and tobacco in a glass. Take out the nkobos and throw the liquid on the ground as this will absorb the negative influence and it will not remain in the house or with anyone of the house. In this sign Cobayende speaks directly and says that the person suffers from melancholia. It is likely that the person has tried to commit suicide. If so tell the client that if he tries again he can be sure to suffer greatly before he dies and he will live long enough to regret it. This is guaranteed. He has many nightmares and suffers from poor health, in particular stomach troubles. He speaks too much. He is a busybody and a gossiper. This brings many troubles to his life and has caused the emnity of someone who desires some kind of revenge. Be careful with negative influences. Cross yourself three times. If it falls in a positive orientation give a rooster to the paleros prenda after being cleansed with it. The cleansing can also be done with smoked fish, jutia, toasted corn or honey. These items are then placed inside the rooster. It is also possible to make a cleansing with a pigeon which is then released. Make a bath with herbs of Cobayende, cologne water, three pinches of tobacco and then pray to the sun. This prayer should be said in the morning at daybreak for the best results. If it falls in a negative orientation you need to cleanse the person with a piece of beef which is placed at the feet of Lucero and stabbed with a knife. It is then covered in cacao butter or shea butter. Wrap it in a piece of jute sack. Do this to overcome this mark.

JURA! THE PACT & THE ROAD

This word, *Jura!* Swear! is burned into the mind of everyone who goes through the rayamento of Tata Nganga. It is a crucial moment where the paradox of unification is absorbed, whether you realize it or not at the time. Palo Mayombe is about solitude. It is the solitude of a unique birth under the wings of Saturn who shields the pact from the nocturnal eyes of the Sun. It is a single triple flame finding birth under the deadly light of the Moon. The Tata and the nfume become one in the nganga. Blood to bones, word to word, fire to fire...the means of unification. The *rayamento*, the cutting, seals and cements the mystical union between living and dead, where the dead come to life and the living die in the vessel, the nganga.

This is a journey without end; it is a single step towards infinity and the embrace of kalunga, nfinda, mpemba and Nzambi. And it is with the cold sister of Kalunga the journey often begins, in the ice cold embrace of Mama Chola who tempts and tempers the Tata to be. In her most raw and direct manifestation she is nocturnal ice and she will penetrate to your bones and demand courage. This is not a meeting with the healing waters, but the waters that build courage, the waters that make you able to receive the fire, the waters of bitterness and vengeance.

The Tata to be is then taken to the Ceiba. This is most important. Here the confrontation with Nsasi takes place, the creative power of the world, lighting itself as he shows himself in the nfinda. At the Ceiba the body is marked by the proper firmas as the Ceiba and the ntoto is marked. The blessing of Ceiba/Nsasi is to gain the blessing of Nzambi. Here you become blind to the world and the gaze is directed inward, to the darkness within that is about to burst out in flames. At the Ceiba the attention of Nkuyu is also tempted forth and enters into the pulse of earth and blood. This marks the last moment of life and the first moment of death. Cobayende flashes forth and stays as a hovering shadow, your guide in the kingdom of Centella. Here Zarabanda lifts his blade and sends you to your death while the fires of Nsasi and Lukankazi blaze forth from the gates. Nkuyu, ever present, unleashes his herds of dead lights from the four quarters and there you stand, in the field of death. It is here the newborn Tata gives up his breath and resurrects with his nfumbe – and together they become nganga. The moment of resurrection is a banquet for the dead. Light flashes forth from blood and bones in this most marvelous garden of unearthly light and power as the new warrior is born. The resurrection is one of light and pain. It is after all a pact as a warrior that is taken – and the courage demanded from Mama Chola must be demonstrated. The newborn Tata is given his prenda, his precious – he is being given himself in a resurrected state. A bond of blood, oath and bonds are made and the one flows into the other giving death to the living and life to the dead. The Tata upon receiving his nganga becomes the living embodiment of centuries of wisdom, a spiritual warrior of honor, dedication and merit. I dare say that if a palero has been done correctly his words never fail and his sense of responsibility and courage inspires others. The Tata Nganga went through the greatest fear, death – and is still alive. Fear will be no more – in its place is honor and dignity.

You who went through this would recognize what is hidden in plain sight and you who believe Palo Mayombe is just some intense form of black magic should think again. Palo Mayombe is about bonding with ancestral memory and it is about entering into an exchange with the dead. I can't help seeing Palo Mayombe as an insistence on maintaining the natural bond between the dead and the living. Its sinister reputation is largely born from the ancestral neglect so prevalent in the modern world.

Traditionally prendas were made in three-legged iron cauldrons. This triplicity we find replicated in the heart of the prenda, so it does not really matter if a terracotta cauldron is used in place of the iron cauldron. The metaphysical aspect is that the triplicity of the vessel coincides with the triplicity of the Tata (soul, body and mind) and generates a union symbolized by the trident, the goose foot, the witch's foot or the veve of the marassa in Vodou. It is a union involving a crossing of the worlds. The points of the Yowa cosmogram meet and melt. As such it becomes a marriage, a contract, not to be forfeited. A marriage can turn cold but is never broken — from the perspective of the inner dynamics of Palo Mayombe. It is a demanding path, it is a pact without divorce.

The nganga is fed with tobacco and strong liquors. The alcohol and the tobacco aid in altering the perception of nfumbe and Tata in conformity with *ntoto* and bring ecstasy to take shape, whether quiet or violent. You and the nfumbe are one by the virtue of the prenda and the prenda attracts hosts upon hosts of Nkuyu's spirit denizens. They can come and work through your body and they can come through dreams. The state of dream, *ndozi*, is the state that corporeal and non corporeal intelligences share. The better your marriage works the better you will discern between your spirit guides and intrusive influences for good or for ill. The path the palero has chosen is one where he serves as an oracular mouthpiece for a great collective of ancestral wisdom. It comes with a certain duty to himself and his closest community. The palero seeks to make life more understandable for himself and his community — and through this, better.

Contrary to popular beliefs that see the palero as a mischievous and malevolent creature, he should be in virtue of his transformation a liminial being who holds in his hands the scales of life and death. By walking with the dead he should help the living — but most certainly this knowledge can also help the living find death and pandemonium. After all, the palero lost his fear of death — and herein is found the kernel of malefica coming from transgression alone. By losing fear a certain hostility towards any lack of courage develops in some paleros, and this in turn spawns misanthropy to such an extent that the life of a coward is deemed worthless. Knowledge of death, not only this — but being death; to give or retain this is a grace and a curse freely available to the mature palero. It is here the greatest challenge enters, this is the twain blade of Palo Mayombe, to balance this dark flame of death against compassion. It is here some paleros fail and fall prey to the sinister inclinations that give Palo Mayombe a rather cruel reputation centered around a palero lacking mercy or good will.

Prayers and mambos make up the liturgy of the palero, but I have found that over time improvisations rising from the heart do tend to manifest in greater abundance.

Lydia Cabrera managed to collect a number of useful mambos and prayers, some of these are presented here, together with other prayers and calls handed down orally. Cabrera's collection seems to be older and linguistically truer to the kikongo language. Knowing that some paleros have suffered from a lack of information, I present here a corpus of useful mambos and prayers that have proven effective:

Greeting the prenda together with godchildren:

Tata	*Jura a Dio Mambi?*
Response	*Dia Nzambi!*
Tata	*Jura a Dio Mambi?*
Response	*Dia Nzambi!*
Tata	*Nganga kuna Yombe*
Response	*Mayombe!*
Tata	*Nfumbi kuna nkongo*
Response	*Nkongo!*
Tata	*Nfumbi kuna nkongo*
Response	*Nkongo!*
Tata	*Nfumbi kuna nkongo*
Response	*Nkongo!*

Greeting the prenda in solitude:

> *Aguiri Nkutu Aguiri Ndinga Mpangui Emboa de Acocan*
> *Bendicion Nsambi*
> *Bendicion Nfumbe*
> *Bendicion Nganga*
> *Wiriko Nganga*
> *Kimbindo Tata Nganga (complete name of palero, prenda and rama)*
> *Licencia to los nfumbe que kuenda munanso kongo*
> *Licencia to los nfumbe que kuenda ntoto nzo (name of munanso/rama)*
> *Licencia (name of prenda)*
> *Licencia (Tatas/Yayas of your rama)*
> *Licencia (name of godfather)*
> *Licencia to lo que kuenda ntoto (name of rama)*
> *Nsala Malecum Malecum Nsala*

When you enter the Munanso:

> *Burunkisa nganga*
> *Nguangara nkunia*
> *Munanfua monunkuame*
> *Tata ndibilongo tuyembere*

The Kimbisa Crede:

> *Tendundu*
> *Qiuenpunguele*
> *Mani masango*
> *Nsilan banza*
> *Mandie*
> *Sese mandie*
> *Bican bioco*
> *Bigan diame*
> *Ndilicuame*
> *Nsambi ndiganga*

For the Knife:

> *Cabanga tengue yaya*
> *Pian kilanga*
> *Tala moko*
> *Nganga nkisi*
> *Nkita mulanga*
> *Ngungu nsanguila*
> *Sogulo basula*
> *Cuenda muino*
> *Mbanzo*
> *Nmusi naba*
> *Nguenguere*

When you enter the Nso:

> *Nso Munanso*
> *Cuenda marlolo*

Salutations to the Nganga:
(Can also be used to salute Kadiempembe/Lukankazi)

> *Sambia mpungu, vititi losa*
> *Tava sili, monopanibele*
> *Machuco congo, Lunguanda buengue*

Chant for attack with Mariwanga:

> *Yo tengo nguerra*
> *Nganga yo te ñama*
> *Mariwanga viti colorá*
> *Vititingo ven acá*
> *Nganga vite colora*

To invite the Nfuri to eat:

> *Vamo lo convite Sáuro*
> *Vamo a lo convite Saurero*
> *Nvamo lo convite Sáura*
> *Dió Mayombero, asi vamo Saurero*
> *Dió Saurero Vamo Saurero!*

To induce trance and oracles:

> *Nsualo mambi Mambi*
> *Bilanga son judeo*
> *Bilanga pañuelo de luto*
> *Bilanga son (judeo)*

For the elevation of the Nfumbe/Nfuri:

> *Como siempre Nganga mira Maria*
> *Como gana batalla Nganga Maria*
> *Cuji yaya, gane bandera Eh! Maria como siempre gana*

To entice the nganga to work:

> *Nganga yo te ñama*
> *Kasimbirikó*
> *Yo tengo Nguerra*
> *Nganga mío yo te ñama*
> *Nganga ñame kasimbirikó*
> *Ahora vamo a jugá*
> *Yimbirá vamo yimbirá*
> *Yimbirá un poco*
>
> *Kasiro mimo*
> *Traen guerra*
> *Kariso*

Kastiwa traen guerra

Como Nkanga Ndoki
Longuisa ndoki chamalongo
Alándoki alándoki

Kángala munu fuá lombe yaya
Cabildo que you lleva
Nunca falta tragedia

Greeting after completing workings:

Kutere Akutere
Acayó Mboma Longankisi
Yo longa moana

Lé malembe mpolo yakara
Malembe moana nkento
Tu kai sem nguei
Munu kiá munu malembe

When tracing the firma:

Kati kampolo munantoto
Batukandumbe Bakurunda
Bingaramanguei

For works with the Owl and Mama Chola:

Ié lechuza pone huevo en la ceiba
Komayanga
Lechuza mandadero en la sombra
Pasa por Csa Grande manda parte pa la Nfinda
Tronco Ceiba tiene lechuza
De verdá Tronco Ceiba

Padre mio abri kutu Cucha cosa Kabulanga

Ya yangó yo wiri mambo
Yo entro la Nfinda
Casa grande viti luto
Ye yangó. Sieete Hueso son Kalunga
Mbele va a cotá kambiriso

Kalunga cota muruwanda
Embacadero son muruwanda
Kalunga mu kalunga
Cota cota muruwanda

For clairvoyance and entering trance:

Yo aprendi divino cosa malo
Suamito dá yo Lucero
Ya yo Lucero yo mira mundo
La fin del mundo la fin del mundo
Ya yo Luceero brinca la mar
Ya yo ve la cosa mundo
Mi suamito mío yo mira mundo
Mayordomo mío yo mira mundo
Yo voy léjo corré mundo
Yo coge Lucero
Corre mundo
Yo avisa Mayombero

Conguito tu no méngaña
Mira vê la Cosa mala
Misuamito da you Lucero
Yo mira mundo divino
Cosa malo yo vé la cosa mundo

To excite the Nganga to work:

> *Diablo lleva mi casamiento*
> *Ngavilían lleva sombra la fin de mundo*
> *Allá la ceiba to mundo va*
> *Chico grande to mundo va*
> *Chiquito grande to mundo va*
>
> *Pobre yimbi dio wá wá*
> *Pobre yimbi dio*
> *Mira yimbi volando… …*
>
> *Secundina tiene való*
> *Dale való Secundina, dale való*
> *Tu deja tu Nganga Mayombe Nkunga*
> *Dale való, való*
> *Secundina való, tiene való*
>
> *Kiangani Watanga mambo*

To work with the Mpaka (trance):

> *Si tu Nganga como yo*
> *Nganga como yo*
> *Nganga la de allí*
> *Baila mi tambó*
>
> *Grúaté cual Nganga como yo*
> *Grúaté venga cantá aquí*

To get advice from Lukankazi or Centella:

> *Kóngoro makongo toc*
> *Kóngoro makongo toc toc*
> *Kongoro makongo*
> *Kokorí kongo*
> *Yombo se va!*

Song for Tata Nfumbe (Cobayende) to quicken nfumbe:

> *Nfumbe Nfumbe*
> *Munu mata*
> *Paso pobre viejo*
> *Por aquí pasó, por aquí gimió*
> *Por aquí pasó mi kunankisa*
> *Y nadie lo vio... ...*

Another song for Nfumbe:

> *Nfumbe Nfumbe fuiri montá*
> *Fumbe malembe fumbe*
> *Epolipó ndana ndana*
> *Epolipó*

Song for Mari Wanga:

> *Mari Wanga yariri*
> *Bankereré eboré Mari Wanga*
>
> *Sambia Sambia Mpungu*
> *Sá isora muana*

How to prepare a life force offering:

Take the nsunsu and wash its beak and feet with malafo and water. If given to a female nkisi also wash it in perfumes.

Present the nsunsu to the person in question then to the prenda and make a declaration of the reasons for the bird to give up its life. Clean the person with the bird while singing:

Limpialo, limpialo, limpialo mi nganga limpialo

Place the animal on top of the prenda and sing:

Recoge lo malo recogelo recogelo recogelo NN (name of the prenda) recogelo.
Mandalo a Nsambia

You will then take the *mbele mbobo* (little sword i.e. knife) and sing:

Filo filo candango, teremene ngo

While the Tata is doing this everyone present will open their mouth and a cross is marked on their tongue with the knife.

This being done pluck a few feathers from the bird's neck singing:

Talangando, talamate, talangando, talamate

As you puncture the neck with the knife you sing:

Vamo Zarabanda, mbele quiere menga,
quiere menga arriba nganga mbele quiere menga

Then, let the blood fall on the prenda while singing:

Sangre nsala delaila, nganga, difunto uria menga, difunto uria menga

When the blood has finished dripping you pour water over the neck allowing the water to fall into the pot and sing:

Lango berikutu eh, lango berikutu eh, yetu yetu Chamalongo

The same is done with chamba singing:

Malafo Chamba berikutu eh,
malafo Chamba berikutu eh,
yetu yetu Chamalongo

The same is done with aguardiente and you sing:

Malafo mamputo berikutu eh,
malafo mamputo berikutu eh,
yetu yetu Chamalongo

The same is done with dry white wine and you sing:

Malafo sese berikutu eh,
malafo sese berikutu eh,
yetu yetu Chamalongo

The same is done with honey and you sing:

Bunke bunke, mi ganga uria bunke,
mi ganga uria bunke, mi ganga uria bunke

With the knife you proceed to cut off the bird's head by presenting the two sides of the knife singing:

Condongo (cutting edge)
Bribana (non-cutting edge)

Then you totally cut off the bird's head singing:

Corta y corta nsusu, corta y corta nganga nsusu

Remove some of the feathers and place them on the pot while singing:

Nsusu suelta el floron, pegalo a mi nganga

Then more malafo mamputo is sprayed over the nganga and more cigar smoke and even incense may be burned and then the nganga is asked if everything is fine for the sacrifice, if not, by logic you ask what is missing. Then when you have the final positive answer you sing:

Combiti Nsaura que bueno eſta'
que bueno eſta', que bueno eſta'

Then you proceed to dispatching the animal, asking what should be done with it. The meat should be eaten and the wings and feet thrown out the door singing:

Abre Talanquera Munanso, difunto eſta pasando

IV NFINDA

GURUNFINDA'S KINGDOM

This herbarium presents a selection of the rich herbal lore at the disposal of the palero. Though by necessity limited, it does contain descriptions of the use of plants which are toxic, deadly and abortifacients. Most of these plants I know myself, but a few only by reputation – so I am communicating both received and tested wisdom. This means that myself and my publisher withdraw support and responsibility from any uninformed and immature use of the herbarium in this section of the book. We advocate cunning use only, and the maturity needed to request cunning advice when administering any of these natural properties manifesting as shrubs, plants and trees in the form of prepared remedies. We, the author and publisher, are not to suffer any liability for immature and foolish use of Gurunfinda's herbarium. There are several plants here that are very toxic and some even deadly. At all times, show care by either knowing what you are doing or seeking assistance from someone who knows exactly what they are doing. A book can never be considered a guide in these matters.

I must also add that some might find inconsistencies in this list compared to what they have been taught. This is a constant problem, often the result of the same term being used for a wide variety of plant species. What I have done in these cases is to analyse the available options and decide upon the one with the most appropriate properties. Where this has been impossible I have presented all the options and a viable way of seeing the plant or palo.

This being said, the palero is a master of herbs and woods, leaves and sticks. If you show lack of mastery of this domain you are not an efficient palero. It shows that you have discarded all the humbling training involved in the path towards mastery. The palero is the bonemaster that guided by his nfumbe and all mpungo and nkisi (both manifested and invisible) knows how to deal with nature. By nature we mean the forest

– and the forest now borders with society. This expands the demands placed on the palero. He needs to know both the natural law and the civil law. The palero is reborn from nature and works in society. It is nature's healing call to society, it is a call for return and an analeptic remedy.

THE HERBARIUM OF MAYOMBE

Abelmosco (*Hibisicus abelmoschus*). This is a fragrant and musky plant adored by Mama Chola Wengue and Baluande. The oil of its seeds can be used as a most potent perfume for attracting these nkisi. Seeds can also be mixed with coffee and given as an offering to nkisi. It repels insects, contains properties that counteract viperous cardio toxins as well as easing colds and fevers. The plant can be used in bilongos of attraction and is a welcome part of their prenda.

Agogo (*Brugmansia suaveolens*). This is a wonderful cousin of Datura which banishes any form of negativity. Leaves and flowers are excellent for use in the purification of a house, people or anything else. A smoking blend can be used both to facilitate dreaming and also for meditative purposes and for spirit interaction. A small dosage is also good for asthma, pulmonary problems and any internal affliction of the chest. It is a plant most adored by Tiembla Tierra, Nkita and Mama Chola, which generates loving bonds between man and spirit.

Akún (*Persea gratissima*) also known as Avocado is a wonderful tree with many fine properties. Like its relative the laurel it wards off any form of hostility and replaces it with good fortune. It is a great herb/ palo to use in making macutos for luck and to change ones fortune. The leaves are good to use when you want to counter high blood pressure, cholesterol and cardiovascular problems. It is rich in many different vitamins and contains vermifuge properties. It can also be used against vaginal infections and restores the liver. This tree is sacred to most, but adored by Zarabanda, Nkuyu, Baluande and Nsasi.

Amuyo (*Erigeron pusillus*) has interesting medicinal properties and expels parasites and vermin from the stomach. It is also efficient against urinary problems and hemorrhage. Tiembla Tierra takes this plant.

Ancanaá/Ntola (*Manilkara albescens*) is a curious shrub with fivefold symmetry. Its flowers have five petals and its fruits always come in clusters of five. It can be used in works to ward off negativity, to confuse and to sweeten. It is especially attractive for Nsasi and Zarabanda.

Banso/Ortiga (*Tragia gracilis*) is a hardy small plant that thrives in harsh conditions. It is a very effective abortifacient and has the property of instigating quarrels and chaos. The plant's roots can be used to make an mpolo to this effect. It is greatly favored by Centella and Vence Bataya.

Bejuco de Cruz/Palo de Cruz can refer to several plants given the wide range of *bejuco* type of herbs. These can range from vanilla to all of the Brownea genus. It is said to counter venereal diseases and impotence. It is sacred to Cobayende.

Bejuco zarzaparilla (*Smilax domigensis*) was used in the past to purify the blood and to treat veneral diseases as well as working against impotence and in the treatment of skin problems. It was one of the plants used to treat syphilis up to 1910. It has also proven effective in the treatment of leprosy and contains rich amounts of steroids and saponins that can easily be transformed into estrogen and testosterone. It is considered a sinister abortifacient and is slightly toxic. Gurunfinda loves this plant.

Beleloasu (*Trichilia hirta*) a relative of Catuaba (*Trichilia catigua*) is a beautiful shrub also known as broomstick – and properly enough it is applied in works of purification and the expelling of hostile and negative spirits. It also dispels body lice and intestinal vermin. It offers remedies against tumors, asthma and pneumonia. Nkuyu and Nsasi like this plant.

Benkeye (*Erythroxylon confusum*) is another relative of catuaba. It is said that this species contains benzoylmethylecgonine and can aid somewhat in problems with respiration and blood. It is, however, used under the influence of Nsasi where it is turned into an mpolo that is thrown to provoke chaos and quarrels of a more violent kind.

Berikolae (*Pithecellobium unguis-cacti*) is a Mimosa type, relative of Dormideira. It is very thorny; it lives in symbiosis with the yellow shouldered parrot, its fruits being crucial to its survival. It can be used for kidney ailments and to expel kidney stones. It is used under the influence of Mama Chola to create chaos and discord between couples and groups.

Bijaguara/Angico/Yopo (*Anadenanthera colubrina*) contains tryptamine and bufotenine in its seeds. The bark contains wonderful properties and can be used against venereal diseases, bronchitis and all forms of pulmonary and respiratory problems. It can also make part of a regime where one desires to regain a strong immune defense system. It is said to be sacred to Nkuyu, Vence Bataya and Mama Chola and is frequently employed to cause insanity.

Billaca (*Cordia gerascanthus/ecalyculata*) is a tree which lives in symbiosis with insects, providing domiciles for its denizens. It can be used in the treatment of skin diseases, scarring and the healing of wounds. It possesses interesting magical properties and can be used for works of cold revenge. It is a tree much loved by Gurunfinda.

Blwoto (*Heliotropium indicum*) is used medicinally for healing wounds and the skin. Care should be taken when introduced internally. It has proven effective in fighting tumors, but it also contains pyrolizidine alkaloids that can provoke tumors, damage and cause cancer in the liver. It is more frequently used in purging baths.

Bukua (*Abarema glaucum*) is a tree indigenous to Cuba and is considered good for success in business, gambling and love. The Coffee tree (*Gymnocladus dioicus*) can be used as a substitute.

Caguairan (*Copaifera L*) is commonly used to extract copal oil which throughout history has been used for almost every infirmity. It is effective against skin problems, urinary afflictions and carries valuable cosmetic properties and is good against acne. It also helps to heal wounds and exterminate warts. It is sacred to Cobayende.

Calentura (*Asclepias curassavica*) is also known as Blood flower and is said to drain the eyes of people, both of life and envy. This is a remarkable plant that can cure or kill and is a great anti-toxin and expeller of viral intruders in the genital region.

Camaguey/Disoto (*Davilla rugosa*) is good to counter skin rashes and to call upon the spirit of Vence Bataya. This name is also given to the ironwood tree (*Krugiodenderon ferrum*) which is a good purgative and can be used to combat toxins in the blood and malaria. It is a palo that infuriates Mama Chola but works well with Zarabanda.

Cana Brava (*Bambusa vulgaris*), known as bamboo, is particularly important for Nkuyu as a channel for bringing ancestral lights and spirits to earth. Interestingly several Asian cultures believe that humankind emerged from the bamboo. It is frequently applied in works where you seek to bring nuisances to adversaries. It is also sacred to Cobayende. The siliceous fluid that can be extracted from the cane is a good medicine for respiratory illness and asthma.

Capa roja/varia (*Cordia gerascanthus*) is a type of laurel claimed by Nsasi and Centella. It is reputed to attract good luck and can be used in order to dominate a situation and destroy blockages. It also serves for insomnia, nervousness, epilepsy and colds.

Carbonero (Cassia biflora) is a shrub or small tree which tends to divide itself in two and carries aphrodisiac qualities. It is reputed to stir sexual desires and can as such be used in any situation that demands the manipulation of fellings. It is a wonderful shrub to use in works to reunite lovers and in works of a sexual and sensual nature. It can also weakens any fever.

Cardo santo/Cando ere (Argemone mexicana) has toxic properties and can lead to internal bleeding and skin ruptures, so should be treated with care. The seeds have a sedative effect, while the dried plant is analgesic and at times is used post-labor to cleanse the body. It can also be used against colic and fever and has been proved to eliminate diabetes. It is sacred to Cobayende and can be used to manifest golden opportunities where there are none.

Cat's Claw (Momisia iguanæa) is used to combat fevers and cures ailments of the liver. It has most remarkable sorcerous qualities and is under the domain of Centella and Lukankazi.

Cedro/Nkunia menga tuala (Cedreira mexicana/Cupressus lusitanica) is a tree with amazingly protective properties and can be used as a substitute for Palo Dominador. In particular Nkuyu and Nsasi are drawn to this tree. Usually the tree used is the white cedar. The tree was used in the process of embalming in Egypt and King David had the Temple built with the cedars of Lebanon. The oil has a most wonderful effect on the limbic system and opens the brain to otherworldly experiences. It can also be used against venereal diseases, tuberculosis, skin disorders, coughs and hair loss.

Ceiba (Ceiba pentandra) the silk cotton tree is joined in a fervent symbiosis with the honey bee. It is the most important tree in Palo Mayombe and is the king of palos. Its majestic presence evokes humility. It can be used for any kind of work aiming towards stability. It is a great purifier that repels all negative things and installs good fortune wherever it is worked. This is Nsasi's favorite tree and it is also closely connected to Tiembla Tierra. It can be used against fevers, afflictions of the kidneys, venereal diseases and menstrual irregularities.

Ceiba/Palma real (*Roystonea regia*) some call the royal palm Ceiba given its equal importance with the Ceiba proper. The royal palm represents Nsasi but is also synonymous with the serpentine descent — and thus the revelation of secrets. It has properties that can help infections of the eyes, gonorrhea, kidney failure and leprosy.

Chamico (*Datura stramonium*) is a well known sacramental plant. In Palo Mayombe the Datura is mostly used in works to induce insanity and to send nightmares to one's adversaries. It does have good medicinal properties related to bladder, impotence, hemorrhoids and rheumatism. The high levels of the alkaloid Hyoscyamine makes it particularly dangerous if too much is taken as it can lead to coma. The presence of the sedative scopolamine aids this process. So, extreme care must be used when working with this plant. It is a plant sacred to Gurunfinda, Mama Chola and Centella.

Chichicate (*Urera baccifera*) is considered a most vile plant and is used in a wide array of negative workings. Considering that some larger species are reputed to have killed cattle its dangerous reputation is deserved. Most commonly it is used to unleash legions of malefica against a target and is particularly sacred to Mama Chola and Lukankazi. It has good medicinal properties and in a soup made of nettles can expel gallbladder stones, aid in the recovery from tuberculosis and heal ovarian bleeding.

Chinyo (*Merremia tuberosa*) is a relative of ipomea. It can be used to heal gonorrhea, swelling of the intestines, irritation of the eyes and mucus. It belongs to Baluande and Tiembla Tierra and is at times used to sow discord or create movement in a situation.

Chona (*Annona glabra*) also known as alligator apple contains properties that weaken cancer growth. It can be quite invasive and is used to weaken the defenses of an adversary and is frequently applied in bilongos to manipulate court cases. It can also have beneficial effects on tuberculosis, pulmonary troubles, expelling intestinal parasites and worms and also in the healing of burns. It belongs to Vence Bataya and Lukankazi.

Chunue (*Cordia valenzuela*) can be used to treat skin problems. It has properties similar to mango in terms of workings and can be used to influence and dominate situations. It is a wood that brings stability to the nkisi and in particular those of Nkuyu.

Conchita (*Clitoria ternatea*) is a plant that is used as an aphrodisiac and to ease abdominal discomfort and painful periods. It has also proved to work well as an antispasmodic and has antidepressant qualities. It belongs to Mama Chola and Baluande and is used in bindings, workings of attraction and all things sensual.

Cle-kukumenga (*Randia aculeata*) the indigo berry is an evergreen that aids liver recovery and has beneficial effects upon diarrhea and hemorrhage. It belongs to Nkuyu and Baluande and can be used in works of purification and to clear away obstacles.

Cuajincillo (*Prunus myrtifolia*) or cherry has proved to contain benevolent properties for combating cancer, especially of the breast and colon. It also has a most welcome effect on the nervous system and the leaves can be used for calmative and purifying baths to expel nervous conditions and tension. It belongs to Mama Chola and Tiembla Tierra.

Cundeamor (*Momordica balsamina*) is a plant that attracts Cobayende, Vence Bataya, and Zarabanda. It has some very interesting properties. It is at times also named after the saint San Caetano. Its leaves are great medicine against internal parasites, diarrhea and bleeding. A decoction can be made and thrown on the ground to kill vermin and larvae of all kinds and make ones perimeter clean. It also helps fight against fevers and can help expel kidney stones. It heals diabetes and eases rheumatic conditions. It works wonders on the immune system and has lately proven to have positive effect upon cancer. The fruit, or melons as they are called due to their similarity with that fruit, are not edible but toxic and are used for aggressive spells where you seek to harm people in the worst ways.

Dagame (*Calophyllum candidissimum*) or lemonwood has throughout history been popular both in the building of shops and the making of bows and arrows. Its bitter and pungent resin treats ulcers and its leaves are most effective in combatting and in some cases neutralizing diabetes. It is a herb that expels negativity and induces focus and a clear mind. It is sacred to Vence Bataya.

Dioke (*Ambrosia artemisiifolia*) or ragweed is good for baths of purification and cleansing – and for lustral waters in general. The weed can also be gathered into a brush and used to sweep places clean. It heals menstrual disorders, fevers, cramps and diminishes excess mucus. It can also ease the itching of insect bites due to its strong allergenic properties. Hay fever is at times attributed to the pollen of dioke.

Dondoko (*Cestrum nocturnum*) is revealed by the intense sweet scent of lilac which it releases in the night. It has proven to give comfort to those suffering from epilepsy, nervousness and spasms due to the presence of solanine alkaloids. This can also help with nausea, fevers and congestion of liver and kidneys; especially if the sap and berries, in particular the immature green berries are consumed. The palero sees this as a wonderful plant for making baths as it attracts good fortune and carries protective properties. It must be added that the plant is excellent in cases where you seek to create obsession and confusion, in particular in matters of love. It is sacred to Tiembla Tierra, Zarabanda and Mama Chola.

Dormideira (*Mimosa pudica*) is a wonderful thorny bush which has a turbulent relationship with lilies and they should not be planted too close to each other. It is a great remedy for fever, insomnia and headaches. The plant carries the power of domination and is particularly useful in love spells and bindings. It is also good to use if you seek to tangle someone up in messy and frustrating situations.

Dulcamara (*Solanum dulcamara*) the bittersweet nightshade or snake-berry is a relative of belladonna, datura and mandrake, but less toxic – thus not deadly as in the case of some of its other family members. It has proved to be highly effective against swellings, skin problems, pains in the joints and herpes. It can be used in works of control and attack where you seek to dominate more than one person, such as a small community or a family. It is sacred to Cobayende and Vence Bataya.

Doúki (*Gossypiospermum praecox*) is often used in place of true box-wood (or rather the European *Boxus* genus). It has properties that are benevolent in the treatment of hypertension, infections and swellings. It is sacred to Tiembla Tierra and is used in works where you seek to dominate and punish.

Egua (*Gonolobus pubescens*) fortifies the immune system and helps the body build a defense against cancer, but it has no significant effect on an already developed cancer. It also stops the development of syphilis and can be used against hemorrhoids, stomach pains and tetanus. Caution must be taken, as it can have nauseating effects if taken in too large a quantity. It is useful in works of confusion and discord and is sacred to Nkuyu.

Embi (*Aristolochia trilobata*) is an Orchid like vine. It contains moderate amounts of aristolochid acid which in large quantities is toxic to the kidneys. It can provoke cancer growth but also the growth of white blood cells. It can increase metabolism and reduces appetite. It has a long medicinal history and was used in Egypt, in particular to purge the body after childbirth and expel the placenta, hence in European traditional medicine it is often called birthwort. It has antiseptic qualities and Centella is particularly fond of this plant, along with Mama Chola. In Palo Mayombe it is most commonly used as an ingredient in baths of purification and purging. It is an excellent bath to make before embarking on difficult tasks.

Escoba Amarga (*Parthenium hysterophorus*) due to parthenin toxins this can cause respiratory malfunctions. It is a plant used for ritual baths and cleansings, but can also be used in bilongos where you aim to turn good things into mediocre ones. A decoction of the plant can be applied to restore the skin, to fight pimples and ulcers. It has some effect on tumors and headaches, although there are options far better than this plant. It is a plant sacred to Cobayende.

Espartillo (*Sporobolus indicus*) is an invasive weed with relaxant qualities. Mostly used for baths, but can also be used in works with Nkuyu and Nsasi, in particular to manifest them as ndoki.

Ewele Keri (*Cissus trifoliata*) also known as grape ivy is a plant that guards the health of a household if planted at the front and back door of the house. It has proven beneficial in the treatment of skin problems, epilepsy and tumors. Its relative *Cissus verticillta* has for centuries been used for cardiac problems, high blood pressure and stopping convulsions. It is sacred to Baluande and brings health, fortune and clarity of mind.

Fideillo (*Cuscuta americana*) is a convolvulus, a morning glory also known as the Devil's hair due to its invasive and parasitic nature. It can attach to a great variety of plants and takes over the vascular system of the plant host and gradually retracts its own root and lives on in the host. This plant has properties that upon investigation reveal a lycanthropic formulae and it is a plant which is very interesting to use in the more secret workings with the nganga and also in the creation of one. It has proven to have some beneficent effects in restoring the liver and purging the blood of toxins. It is sacred to Nsasi, Lukankazi and Mama Chola.

Fiko (*Erythroxylum vacciniifolium*) is a tree with great aphrodisiac properties. It stimulates blood flow and restores potency. It also stimulates the nervous system and fights fatigue. The plant, also known as catuaba, has proven to have positive effects in the treatment of HIV and related viral afflictions. It is sacred to Zarabanda and is used in works of sexual domination and to ensure success and stability, in particular for new partnerships, whether of love or business.

Finli (*Hura crepitans*) with its spiny grey trunk is commonly used in works of protection and to expel intrusive spirits and people. It has benevolent effects on the circulation of blood and contains hypnotic properties. It is at times used as a component in the sacred drink ayahuasca. It is also known as dynamite tree due to the noise caused when the seed caps are bursting and is sacred to Nsasi and Zarabanda.

Firio (*Indigofera suffruticosa*) is at times used ritually due to its indigo pigments which when fused with clay turn into an intense royal blue color. It can drain the blood of haemoglobin, which speaks of the vampyric tendencies inherent in this plant. It is used in works of purification and is sacred to Baluande – but at heart it binds with Lukankazi.

Flecheo (*Pithecellobium saman*) also called rain tree serves to treat asthma, syphilis, ulcers and wounds. In Palo Mayombe it has diverse uses and is used in funeral rites as well as in bilongos to attract good fortune and to overcome legal issues. The tree is counted as an ancestral tree and serves well as a point of egress with Tiembla Tierra and Gurunfinda.

Frijol refers to a variety of beans and peas. Any kind of beans are good for macutos due to their long historical and spiritual bond to the dead. They are particularly sacred to Cobayende and Zarabanda. In particular, the black beans (*phaseolus vulgaris*) can be used both as offerings and as a means for facilitating communication and manifestation.

Fugwé (*Abrojo tribulus cistoides/terrestris*) is at times used in the mend-iba baths of Abakuá, as a ritual purgative and preparation. It is also used in palo rituals and ceremonies as an agitator for the medium and facilitates receiving the spirit. It has also proven benevolent in restoring muscle tissue and has positive effects on potency and lust. It can cause abortion and is used to expel the placenta. It is a powerful plant that restores the immune system, is good against venereal diseases, skin diseases, tumors and strengthens liver and kidney. It is sacred to all nkisi.

Fumasi (*Elsota virgata*) is used to break spells and against flu, urinary afflictions bronchitis, menstruation, kidney problems, impotence, venereal diseases, nervousness, pains in the joints and sores. It is particularly the root that is useful. It can also be used in works for opening opportunities and is sacred to Vence Bataya and Baluande.

Genjibre (*Zingiber officinale*) or ginger should be well known for its many positive properties and is beneficial in combatting colds, diarrhea and fevers. It also nurtures the body's immune defense. It is a plant/root that is generally excitory and is used in works of protection and when defenses are prepared. It excites Zarabanda, but not always in a good way, so be mindful of this.

Gougoró (*Cinnamomum camphora*) is good against muscular aches and rheumatic pain, but it is also an effective spider and scorpion repellent if smeared on the doors and walls. It has aphrodisiac properties and is a great ward against malefica in general, being purgative in quality. Nsasi, Mama Chola and Centella like this wood and it can be used to entice them to work.

Granada (*Punica granatum*) pomegranate has a rich history through mythology and use. The seeds are a potent tonic for the heart and the fruits skin is a vermifuge. It slows down cataracts if used as an eye potion. It also inhibits the growth of cancer, especially in women and has proven effective against viral and bacterial infections. It is used to banish hostility and negativity, for purifications and in cases where a person is followed by bad fortune to ward off accidents and to chase away the spirits of nightmare. Centella, Baluande, Zarabanda and Nsasi find great delight in this plant.

Groo (*Bucida angustifolia*) is used in Haiti in connection with Trois Bois or Bosseu to make wangas. In Cuba it is mostly used as a remedy against seasickness, but it does contain qualities which make it useful in works of healing and protection, and also to create confusion. It is sacred to Cobayende and Baluande.

Guaney (*Linociera domingensis*) alias Hueso blanco is used as a stimulant and a tonic for the heart. It is a good plant for banishing and expels with great ease the presence of unwanted individuals. It is particularly sacred to Tiembla Tierra and Vence Bataya.

Guaco (*Mikania guaco*) has properties that make it valuable when there is the need to expel ingested bilongos and in general to counter aggresive malefica. It also carriers properties that ameliorate conditions like asthma, fever, insect bites, syphilis and malaria. It is sacred to Gurunfinda and Zarabanda.

Hueso (*Picramnia pentandra*) has been used in the treatment of malaria, dysentery and skin diseases of various kinds; it is a powerful febrifuge and can also be used in the treatment of dengue. Its indigo berries can also be used as a dye. The plant is used to ward off any hostile intrusion and illness. It is very sacred to Cobayende and Centella.

Iggioro (*Beilschmiedia pendula*) is a relative of the walnut and laurel and is at times also known as slugwood as the berries are reminiscent of sloe berries. Moss is drawn easily to this hardy frost resistant evergreen wood. It is used for bilongos and macutos for success, working on the sense of confidence and security of the one who bears it.

Imbi Iye (*Elaphrium simaruba*) is a wood used to make drums in Haiti and has a most intense relationship with garlic, which fortifies its potency. Baths and the most important lustral waters can be made with the aid of this tree. It is rich in the hydrocarbon hexane and serves as an important purifier of the air. It embodies almost universal properties, but is particularly good for countering gout, (the bark) and infusion of its leaves will purge and revitalize the entire body and internal organs. It is particularly sacred to Nkuyu and Cobayende.

Inki (Gymnanthes lucida) is a beautiful wood, mostly used to induce emotional stability in men and nkisi. A medicinal infusion of bark and leaves can be applied to ease muscle pain and to make rheumatic pain more bearable. It belongs to Cubayende and Nkuyu.

Inkita/Cuaba (Amyris balsamifera) is a highly flammable and fragrant wood whose leaves combat most forms of venereal disease and fevers. The oil eleni is extracted from this wood. It is a great attractor of good fortune but the black type attracts more sinister fortunes.

Ise (Pimpinella anisum) or Anise is great against menstrual colics and any form of intestinal infirmities. The presence of phytoestrogen contributes to a weakening of fertility, while in males it has been shown to work beneficially on prostate conditions. It is a plant that draws spirits easily and facilitates true dreaming. It can as easily bring nightmares as ward them off.

Inso/Siguaraya (Trichilia havanensis) is a very important wood, given its protective properties and its ability to mislead any adversary. It is reputed to open roads with as great an ease as it closes roads. It can be used as a medicine against weak kidneys, problems with the bladder, venereal diseases and skin problems. It serves well for all nkisi, but Nsasi takes a certain pride in its qualities.

Kindungo (Capsicum annuum) is known in the wider variety of this genus of peppers. It is a remedy of rejuvenation and combats fevers, asthma, old age and viral infections. In practice both chili peppers and bell peppers are counted in this group and used according to their fierceness. Its properties are both protective and defensive; it serves for expelling and summoning spirits. It is in many ways the power of fire held in your hands and moved by your intent. It is sacred to Nkuyu, Nsasi and Lukankazi.

Kousu (*Stillingia sebifera*) is similar to the Alder and is said to possess properties of rejuvenation. The waxy raisin around the seeds can be used as a tonic to make grey hair white. It has good effects on the kidney and urinary tract and heals skin ulcers. It is an important plant for people in old age to maintain vitality. It is particularly sacred to Cobayende.

Kuakari (*Didymopanax morototoni*) is a very elegant tree and can ease tension and hysteria just as much as it can be used for purifications of an emotional kind or in reverse, creating tension and hysteria. It belongs to Mama Chola.

Kualango Dianputo (*Allium sativum*) or garlic should be a well known ward of illness and malefica, due its powers of bringing what is bad to a halt and welcoming good fortune. In addition to properties of protection it is also good for the kidneys, high blood pressure and infections in general. It is particularly favored by Centella and Cobayende.

Kunino (*Schæfferia frutescens*) is a type of boxwood commonly used to appease, dominate and bind. Decoctions can be made to combat flu, colds and coughs. It serves well for works with Nkuyu and Mama Chola.

Langwe (*Cordia collococca*) is sometimes used to make guitars. It contains properties which combat fever and dropsy. It is a fragile plant and can be used in works where one seeks to weaken the defence and life of an adversary. It is sacred to Centella and Nkuyu.

Leremi (*Securidaca volubilis*) is sometimes used as a wonder medicine for several ailments, but is particularly good for restoration of the liver.

In Palo Mayombe it is under the dominion of Mama Chola and is used to reunite people that have parted because of bilongo. It is as such an anti-bilongo medicine.

Loso (*Oriza sativa*) Rice belongs to Tiembla Tierra and is good for banishing what is bad and attracting good fortune. It supports general health and has a deep ancestral connection. A dietary regime over the course of seven days where one feeds only on rice water and attends to the boveda (see APPENDIX) is bound to unleash rueful vision of one's destiny or address the fears that need to be dealt with that block your progress – these are still a message from the ancestors.

Lunga Kuma (*Zanthoxylum martinicense*) is good against afflictions of the liver and syphilis. The thorns are at times used to make bilongos and macutos for warding off the evil eye. It belongs to Vence Bataya.

Maeri/Gwangango (*Acacia cornigera*) is a most important wood, not only in Palo but also in Vodou and Haitian Masonry where it is said that this was the Tree of Knowledge. Interestingly the wood invigorates manhood, sexual vitality and brings rejuvenation and a youthful energy. Its rich pheromone content might be one reason why male animals in general distance themselves from this tree. This tree lives in complete symbiosis with ants. The thorns on the tree serve as houses for ants who in return defend the tree. It is very sacred to Zarabanda and Vence Bataya.

Macusey Macho (*Philodendrum lacerum*) with its young leaves that looks like dragon's heads treats arthritis, sores and toothache. It is a most virtuous plant to use in works of protection and Vence Bataya comes speedily at its request.

Maguey is said to be *Yucca gloriosa* but I believe this is incorrect, it must be its relative Peregun (*Dracena*) as this one, in contrast to the Yucca, does not irritate the skin but creates purity and enables you to

gather your mind into serenity and dedication. It is a plant of Vence
Bataya.

Male (*Cucurbita maxima*) or pumpkin is well-known in contemporary Halloween celebrations and has a connection to the waking dead.
It is a vermifuge, fights inflammation and serves as a heart tonic. The
seeds are good for the marrow and heart. Its uses in Palo Mayombe
are various, the container can serve as a repository of bilongo and the
seeds can form part of bilongos and mpolos. The seeds can be charged
and thrown in conformity with intent. It is sacred to Cobayende and
Luknakazi.

Manlofo (*Ficus religiosa*) used as a remedy for granular lids and pan-
nus. It has a long history in the East: a fig grove is considered a place
where sacred awakening can occur. It is a popular wood to use when
making macutos of Nkuyu and serves well for banishings of all sorts
and to solidify protection and attract good fortune. It has properties
that fight cholera, inflammation, fever, vaginal infections, pimples,
weak nerves and smallpox. It is an important wood for initiations and
essential for funerals as it is given a dramatic elevation in works with
the nganga.

Mansagro (*Macfadyena unguis cacti*) belongs to Vence Bataya and can
be used to separate and create chaos amongst friends. See also *Cat's
Claw*.

Masere (*Myrica cerifera*) is also known as bayberry and was used
in the past to manufacture wax candles. It can be used against bacterial infections, inflammation and asthma. It has also been used against
cholera, typhoid and to fortify the immune defence system. It serves
as an antibiotic and is a quite violent abortifacient. It belongs to Mama
Chola, Lukankazi and Tiembla Tierra.

Mastuerzo (*Lepidium virginicum*) is used to attract love and belongs to Baluande and Tiembla Tierra. Remarkably it is a plant of Saturn that draws the attention of the Sun.

Mayanda (*Carthamus tinctorius*) is used for afflictions of the uterus, menstrual pains, fever, measles, wounds and sores. It dramatically increases metabolism and ignites energy. It can be used profitably as a war bath dedicated to Zarabanda or to Mama Chola.

Mbala (*Ipomea batatas*) commonly known as sweet potato has properties that fight dengue and malaria and also help to control blood sugar, so it is good for diabetes. It induces stamina and strength and is used for works of stabilization and keeping good fortune. It is sacred to Vence Bataya, Zarabanda and Mama Chola.

Mbota (*Cordia alba*) serves to diminish cramps and tumors. It can be used in bilongos of binding. It is sacred to Mama Chola and Cobayende.

Mbuni/Coffee (*Bunchosia nitida*) is a very hardy wood used in healing rituals, cleansings and against the evil eye. In colonial times the seeds were dried, roasted and made into a simulacrum of coffee. It has great defensive properties and belongs to Zarabanda and Cobayende.

Mechuso (*Ocimun basilicum*) is great for blisters, bad breath, difficult labor, intestinal parasites, unrest, and slow production of milk. It serves to banish negativity, and in workings of love and binding spells. It can also attract good fortune and be used for cleansing of the soul as much as rashes of the skin. It has a most harmonious relationship with coconut water and belongs to Mama Chola and Cobayende.

Monchunto/Copaiba (*Copaifera officinalis*) is antifungal and is a fierce warrior against cancer and tumor. It is also beneficial in combating venereal diseases, incontinence and skin disorders. It can be used in works of attack and protection and belongs to Nsasi and Cobayende.

N*demba* (*Sesamum indicum*) sesame seeds, for anaemia and constipation. Taboo for nkisi, they ward off negativity. Considered to be the oil of the sun and therefore intrusive in the realm of death. Sesame oil was considered a substance of immortality in several ancient cultures and of course, to give immortality to what is already awakened in a secret manner under the moon would counter its existence.

N*duambo* (*Gossypium arboreum*) is good against urinary infections and infections in general. It is a good tonic to give during pregnancy and also eases stomachaches, fatigue and headaches. It is good for all nkisi as it is a wonderful bath of purification that expels death and negativity. It is sacred to Tiembla Tierra and Baluande.

N*dukora* (*Tetracera volubilis*) is used for all forms of chest ailments and asthma. It heals spider bites and has antiseptic properties. It has also been used against gonnoreah. It is particularly sacred for Mama Chola and Centella and can be used to generate malefic situations in a household.

N*buembo* (*Batatas crassicaulis*) can be used against chesty colds, fevers, flu, itches and wounds. It has defensive properties, but is little used. It belongs to Zarabanda and Nkuyu.

N*fei* (*Agapanthus africanus*) has proven to be effective against tumors and is used in baths of purification and to stir up situations. It belongs to Baluande and Tiembla Tierra.

N*gúngo* (*Kallistroemia maxima*) or sagebud is most efficient in works of purification, cleansings and to reverse spells. It is also good against asthma, tumors and ulcers and is most sacred for Tiembla Tierra and Cobayende.

N*kafo Kibulo* (*Solanum havanese*) is a good remedy against general afflictions of the eyes, intestinal worms and is used in a great variety of rituals and bilongos for many purposes. It seems that the plant is quite mercurial in nature and adapts in conformity with what else is added. It is sacred to Gurunfinda, Zarabanda and Nkuyu.

Nkunia (*Datura suaveolens*) is excellent for binding and to bring people together, especially the root. Tiembla Tierra and Mama Chola claim this plant which is excellent for ritual baths of attraction and the increase of animal magnetism. See also *Agogo*.

Nontori (*Heteropterys laurifolia*) is a curious plant – like an unholy cousin of laurel – which can be applied in works of bindings. It has obsessive qualities and heats the blood. It belongs to Mama Chola and Tiembla Tierra.

Npoti (*Hippocratea volubilis*) is a close relative to the *banisteriopsis caapi* which is dominant in the sacred drink known as ayahuasca. It is a potent remedy against chest ailments and snake bites. It is used in workings of prosperity and to fortify ones luck. It is also useful in workings where there is a need to temper the medium and remove resistance. Tiembla Tierra and Nsasi are particularly fond of this plant.

Nyouyole (*Gouania polygama*) is a most important plant recognized by the woody spine on the end of each branch. It has violent purgative properties and is at times confused with the proper mimic dogwood (the *Cornacea* genus signifies being horned/thorny) which ties it in with the dogs of Hecate and travelling between the worlds. It has black berries abundant with solanum and is as such also called Black nightshade. The wood itself is extremely hardy and strong. This plant is at times said to be the blood of Gurunfinda and I must say that this is very revealing of his qualities. Knowledge of this herb is knowledge of Gurunfinda.

Oline (*Chenopodium ambrosoides*) also known as the Jesuit's tea and the herb of the Holy Mary has a taste similar to fennel and anise, albeit with an additional note of bitterness. It is said to bring a cure in the betterment of tension, anemia, tumors, parasites, lack of lactation in mothers, malaria and hysteria and in giving a boost to the immune system. It is also a most powerful vermifuge. It is a good ward against negativity and has the power of annoying adversaries and even destroying them. It is sacred to Vence Bataya, Mama Chola and Lukankazi.

Pangua (*Nicotinia tabacum*) or tobacco has a wide array of beneficial properties. It is a plant that stimulates the central nervous system and contributes to the release of several neurotransmitters, such as serotonin and dopamine – but also growth hormones. It is a good plant for maintaining male strength and combats cancer growth by fortifying the immune system. It can also be used as a sedative and anti spasmodic, its leaves can be applied to insect bites and scorpion stings. It can be turned into a tonic for the lungs and as a vermifuge. It is an ever present part of the cult, but is particularly sacred to Gurunfinda, Nsasi and Lukankazi.

Peppers (*Piper aduncum/Piper nigrum*) are good for purification, blood toxins, gonorrhea, stomach ailments, and liver problems. Dispels or expels conflict. Sacred to Cobayende and Zarabanda. See also: Kindungo.

Peregrina (*Kalanchoe aegyptiaca*) is a family of plants reputed to bring good fortune and abundant blessings. It is frequently used for gastric problems and an efficient cough syrup can be made from it. It is a wonderful purifier and dispeller of negativity. It is sacred to Baluande.

Plantano (*Musa paradisiacal*) or plantain is associated with long life and has the ability to chase away afflictions of all kinds and of sweetening the ancestors. It can be used against gangrene, problems with the menstrual flow, as a vermifuge and against syphilis. Though more recognized as a global food resource it truly possesses great medicinal qualities. Plantain is generally good as an offering but not the lilac ones, which are taboo – although they can be used in particularly nasty workings with Cobayende and Centella. The plant is sacred to all nkisi.

Rompe Zaraguey/Abre camino (*Eupatorium polyanthes/Vernonia polyanthes*) has many wonderful properties and has been used against dengue, malaria, infections, migraine, bronchitis and flu. It can be used as a general tonic for regenerative purposes, but care should be taken as long term use can damage the liver. It is a much used plant, both for purifications and protection. It attracts good fortune and is indispensable for the prenda. It can also be used in bilongos concerning love and justice with good results. It belongs to Tiembla Tierra, Baluande and Vence Bataya.

Sandu (*Cocos nucifera*) also known as coconut, is commonly used for cleansing baths and to calm down agitated people and prendas. Its medicinal qualities are however amazing. It works wonders for the skin; it can be used as a tonic for the heart and reduces fever. It can also aid in digestive problems. In Palo Mayombe, the husk is used to make the chamalongos and it is a fruit desired by all nkisi.

Seikon (*Acalypha diversifolia*) is used as a cure for afflictions of the digestive system, regenerative system, against hemorrhoids and for cleansings. It is seen as a good plant for the restoration of vitality and strength. It belongs to Baluande, Tiembla Tierra and Cobayende.

Sekuse (*Philodendron bipinnatifidum*) is used as a vermifuge tonic. It is a caustic tonic and can also be used against rheumatism and ulcers. It is an energizer in bilongos of the more ndoki type and restores male vigor. It is sacred to Lukankazi and Cobayende.

Sigua (*Celosia cristata*) is anti-bacterial, astringent, and is good for any kind of bleeding. It is used in works to attract confidence and thus it brings a certain allure to the person who uses it, enabling him or her to better manipulate a given situation. It is sacred to Nkuyu, Gurunfinda and Nsasi.

Sucui (*Ilex montana*) is a holly with great properties for restoring the liver's health and to fortify and energize the body. It is a good tree to plant outside ones nzo as its mere presence purifies and protects. It is very sacred to Tiembla Tierra.

Sunsumie (*Acacia farnesiana*) is amongst the more effective treebarks in curing malaria. It is also an excellent skin tonic and against diarrhea, gangrene and nervousness, having sedative properties. It is used to bring chaos and anxiety to ones adversaries. It is sacred to Centella, Cobayende and Mama Chola.

Tongo (*Leonitis nepetifolia*) serves well against high blood pressure, herpes, anaemia, fevers and muscle aches. It can be used in workings where you seek to confuse and mislead adversaries and also to call people to find their way to you. It is at times referred to as lion's ladder or St. Francis' ladder. It can be smoked to induce a sedative and slightly hypnotic state sacred to Gurunfinda, Tiembla Tierra, Nsasi and Nkuyu.

Topiá (*Acacia gliricidia sepium*) is sometimes called Palo Cacao and is a multi purpose tree. An infusion made from the bark and leaves will serve as a powerful repellent of external parasites and insects. It is also used to cure bruises and colds. It is excellent for any kind of macutos and is said to give 'sight'. It attracts prosperity and repels negativity. It is sacred to Vence Baya and Zarabanda.

Totoi (*Commelina virginica*) has anti-hypertensive properties and can be used as a tonic for the skin. It is used for purifications and repulsing negativity. It belongs to Baluande.

Touje (*Polianthes tuberosa*) is a very attractive plant for the nfumbe. It is said to calm down nfuri and make nfumbe more serene. It stimulates the medium and can be used in the misa espiritual to great advantage. It is a good heart tonic and is used in works of peace and prosperity; it brings tranquility and a more lofty spirituality in its peaceful and aphrodisiac potency. It is sacred to Baluande, Tiembla Tierra and Mama Chola.

Túanso (*Turbina corymbosa*) Women's distress, pregnancy, purification of body, mind and house. Tuanso is also the name given to *Terminalia catappa* which carries similar properties but also expels intestinal worms and parasites and attracts good fortune. Túanso is sacred to Tiembla Tierra.

Tufiolo (*Coffea arabica*) is a well known drink which is a recurring offering for nfumbe and is also used with great benefit in many forms of bilongo adding the element of strength and direction to any kind of working. It is sacred to all nkisi and important for all the nfumbe.

Vergonzosa (*Papaver somniferum*) or the poppy has an amazing array of healing properties. It can with great benefit be used against asthma, insomnia, mania, aches, fever, nervousness and infections. It is used in the most diverse bilongos, in workings of love and domination and also to bring insanity and confusion to the enemy. It belongs to Mama Chola and Vence Bataya.

Wangara (*Sapindacaea/Serjania/Litchi*) this class of plants can be represented by Litchi and this as its close relatives are also known as Bejuco Batalla, Palo Batalla and Vencebatalla. The husks of the fruits and the bark can serve to combat diarrhea and the seeds can be dried and turned into a powder that can be used to ease inflammations, especially of the testicles. It is a wood used in works of victory and attack. It belongs to Nkuyu and Vence Bataya.

Waniko (*Thunbergia fragrans*) is used against headaches and insomnia. It can also be turned into an effective salve to treat wounds. It can be used in works of confusion and to attack a person. It can also be used to cause accidents in a person's life. It belongs to Zarabanda, and Vence Bataya.

Yena (*Petiveria alliacea*) is another wonder plant that can be used against fever, malaria, headaches, venereal diseases, rabies, and poisonings of various kinds. It is a potent abortifacient and is also good against toothache and related pains, as well as skin disease. It is an excellent repeller of bilongos worked against the household and also against bats due to its very prominent putrefactive qualities. It has been shown to have good effects in the treatment of Alzheimers. It is sacred to Mama Chola, Cobayende, Gurunfinda and Zarabanda.

Yongoso (*Helianthus annus*) is better known as sunflower. It is a great plant with many wonderful qualities. It is good against insect bites, fevers, malaria and pains in general. It is considered to be almost as potent as laurel in works of victory by attracting good fortune. It is sacred to Zarabanda and Baluande.

Yukula/Caoba (*Swietenia mahagoni*) has antibacterial properties and can be used to cure anaemia, cleanse the blood of toxins, malaria and fever. It is a well known noble wood and is used in works of domination and punishment. It is particularly sacred to Vence Bataya, Mama Chola and Nsasi.

Yumbe (*Capsicum baccatum*) is cayenne pepper and has in addition to the uses of other peppers been considered excellent in bilongos of attack. The fruit itself in these cases serves as the vessel for the bilongo. It is great against fevers menstrual problems, asthma, and colds and the cayenne is particularly favored by Lukankazi and Mama Chola.

A GATHERING OF THE MOST COMMON PALOS

These are the most useful and known palos. Palos are used as mpolos, or as they are in bilongos, and to make the nganga. This is a list of their qualities and under whose dominion they lie.

Palo Alana, see *Palo Ayúa*.

Palo Algarrobo/Flecheo (*Pinthecellobium saman*) or rain tree is used in funeral rites/death spells and to overcome legal issues and attract good fortune. It belongs to Cobayende, Centella and Nsasi.

Palo Amargo (*Picramnia reticulate*) is good in cases of alcoholism (some paleros use it in their drinks to counter the alcoholic tendencies the cult seems to provoke), arthritis, stomach ailments, to expel witchcraft and cause despair. It belongs to Nsasi and Zarabanda.

Palo Amarillo (*Bocconia frutescens*) is a vermifuge and is sacred to Lukankazi, Mama Chola and Vence Bataya.

Palo Ayúa (*Zanthexylum martinicense*) is said to be a 'savior' amongst trees and is often applied in works of expelling negativity and also *rompiementos*, which is a form of exorcism. It can be used with all nkisi, especially the male ones.

Palo Blanco (*Simarouba flauca*) treats diabetes and dysentery. It is a wood that banishes negativity and belongs to Gurunfinda.

Palo Bobo/Cimmarona (*Annona glabra*) weakens the victim. It neutralizes toxins, heals tuberculosis and pulmonary afflictions. It is a vermifuge and strong decoctions can neutralize the effects of other medicines. It belongs to Zarabanda and Centella.

Palo Bomba (*Xilopia glabra*) is a sinister palo that causes internal bleeding. Sacred to Nsasi, Vence Bataya.

Palo Bronco (*Malpighia biflora*) is a protective palo that eases pains during menstruation and can be used against hair loss. It belongs to Tiembla Tierra.

Palo Caballero (*Phorandendron rubrum*) is a great protector against the evil eye and belongs to Nsasi.

Palo Caja (*Allophyllus cominia*) has great protective properties and is frequently used in bilongos and macutos. It can also be used against high blood pressure, tuberculosis and intestinal problems. It belongs to Nsasi.

Palo Ceniso (*Pithecollobium obovale*) is used in works of balance and to bring stability into ones life. It belongs to Tiembla Tierra.

Palo Chango, see *Palo Real*.

Palo Cuaba (*Amyris balsamifera*) is important for vititi, the sight. Anointed with libations, waters or blood it confers the power of invisibility and can also be used to relocate lost things. It is the treasure hunter amongst the palos and belongs to Gurunfinda and Nkuyu.

Palo Cahchimba (*Aralia capitata*) is very protective against hostile spiritual influences and belongs to Nsasi.

Palo Café (*Amaioua corymbosa*) can be used as incense with powerful expelling qualities. It is sacred to Nsasi, Zarabanda and Tiembla Tierra.

Palo Caliente (*Copaiba*) is antifungal and is a fierce warrior against cancer and tumors. It is also beneficial in combating venereal diseases, incontinence and skin disorders. It can be used in works of attack and protection and belongs to Nsasi and Cobayende.

Palo Cambia Voz (*Schaefferia frutescens*) is a marvelous plant to use in works where you need someone to change their mind, or to distort a court case. It is great against flu, impotence and possesses aphrodisiac qualities, making it great in bilongos of love. It belongs to Mama Chola.

Palo Caimitillo (*Chrysophylum oliviforme*) is a great wood for victory and stability. It can also treat diabetes and fever. It belongs to Centella.

Palo Caimito (*Chrysophyllum cainito*) can be used to treat hemorrhage, sores, diseases of the mouth and stomach. It not only has protective properties but tends to return bilongos back to their sender. It belongs to Cobayende and Nkuyu.

Palo Cenizo (*Pithecollobium obovale*) is used to induce stability and belongs to Tiembla Tierra.

Palo Clavo (*Eugenia caryophyllata*) is used to expel ingested witchcraft, it is a vermifuge and can also treat diabetes, problems with digestion, and aches in general. It is sacred to Zarabanda.

Palo Cochino (*Tetragastris balsamifera*) is used against colics and fevers and is a great purifier. It is sacred to Nsasi and Baluande.

Palo Curbana (*Canella alba*) is used to attract love, good fortune and prosperity. It can also be used for colds, menstrual problems and digestion. It is sacred to Mama Chola and Baluande.

Palo Diavolo. Given the great variety of palos called *diavolo* this is more a reference to trees with specific characteristics, like the devil's shoestring, alder wood, yew and poisonous thorny shrubs and trees. A frequent candidate is the Jamaican Caper Tree (*Capparis cynophal-lophora*). It is a risky palo to use as it attracts negativity. It belongs to Nkuyu and Lukankazi.

Palo Dominador is a name given to several shrubs and trees that all share hardiness and most of them are quite elastic and sappy when fresh, like the sambucus, which is a good candidate for the Palo Dominador. It belongs to Vence Bataya and Zarabanda.

Palo Guaco/Climbing Hempweed (*Mikania codifolia*) also known as viper worth is an important palo used to counteract bilongos, especially if they have been ingested. It belongs to Zarabanda and Gurunfinda.

Palo Guairafe/Guará (*Cupania cubensis*) is an essential palo due to its purifying properties. It belongs to Centella.

Palo Guasima/West Indian Elm (*Guazuma tomentosa*) possesses wonderful healing properties and belong to Nkita and Baluande.

Palo Guayacán/Yunkaguá (*Gaicum officinale*) is a strong and solid wood which is sometimes taken as Palo Dominador. And indeed it is a great dominator possessing good guiding qualities. It belongs to Zarabanda, Nsasi and Vence Bataya.

Palo Guitarra (*Citharexylum caudatum*) or juniper is a wood that brings victory, serenity and also opens up a strong connection with the nfinda. It has great antiseptic and diuretic qualities. It belongs to Gurunfinda and Vence Bataya.

Palo Hediondo (*Cassia emarginata*) is important in rites of passage and is sacred to Nkuyu and Nsasi.

Palo Jaguey/Palo Yo Puede Mas Que To (*Fícus crassinervia/trigonata*) is the fig that gives green fruits. It is crucial in all prendas due to its stabilizing and putrefactive properties. It is used in works to overcome legal problems and it is a potent attractor of good fortune. It belongs to Nsasi and Zarabanda.

Palo Jeringa (Moringa oleifera) is a most important wood. It is the great restorer amongst the palos. It restores passion and strength. It is an aphrodisiac and can be used against asthma, cold, fever, vertigo, tumors, hysteria and it purifies water in dramatic ways. It belongs to Baluande.

Palo Jicotea is commonly a type of the *Castanea* genus. It has great protective qualities, and is considered to be the shield of palos. It is sacred to Vence Bataya.

Palo Malambo, see *Palo Curbana.*

Palo Manga (Mangifera) is a royal tree that is used in works of protection and to secure shaky situations. This palo is 'the rock' of the sticks. It belongs to Vence Bataya and Tiembla Tierra.

Palo Monte (Malpighia biflora) is an important protective palo. It is sacred to Gurunfinda and Tiembla Tierra.

Palo Moro (Psychotria brownei) is an excellent wood for bindings of all sorts. It is sacred to Mama Chola.

Palo Moruro (Pithecolobium arborem) is frequently used to make the chicherikú and is used in bilongos of vengeance, to shake someone's stability and to send nightmares. It is sacred to Nkuyu, Centella and Lukankazi.

Palo Mulato (Exothea paniculata) is a good putrefactive wood and can be used as incense. It belongs to Mama Chola.

Palo Papo (Fagelia bitaminosa) is a good wood to affix bilongos in; it is often used as a 'fixative' in macutos. It belongs to Mama Chola.

Palo Ramon (*Trophis racemosa*) is similar to Palo Moruro, but with more dominant qualities. It is unbeatable in its power to dominate spirits and can also be used to increase lactation in women. It is an essential palo and is particularly sacred to Nsasi, Zarabanda and Vence Bataya.

Palo Rayo (*Parkinsonia aculeate*) is a wood used to provoke adversaries and can be used to heal epilepsy and fever. It is sacred to Nkuyu and Mama Chola.

Palo Real/Palma Real (*Roysonea regia*) is all about strength and energy; the balanced sum of nature. It belongs to Nsasi.

Palo Rojo comes in several forms, but frequently African Coralwood (*Pterocarpus soyauxii*) is used though it can refer to Pau Brasil (*Caesalpinia echinata*). It has the potency to envigorate and open us to victory. It is sacred to Zarabanda, Nsasi and Gurunfinda.

Palo Rompehueso (*Casearia sylvestris*) is good in all cases where one seeks to overcome obstacles. It fights diseases ardently and gives relief from burns, wounds and afflictions of the skin. It belongs to Zarabanda, Nsasi and Centella.

Palo Santo (*Gilibertia arborea*) for works of elevation. Also known as *amyris balsamifera* it is used in works to change situations and in particular people's minds, hence it is also called Cambia Voz. Also known as *ocotea foeniculacea,* which holds similar properties. It is sacred to Nsasi and Tiembla Tierra.

Palo Tengue (*Poeppigia procera*) is a most respected palo that is used for almost anything. It is great for stability and protection. It is sacred to Vence Bataya and Nsasi.

Palo Tosino/Palo Torcido (Mouriri valenzuelana) is used to twist someone's luck and belongs to Mama Chola and Nkuyu.

Palo Tocino (Acacia paniculata) is used against gonorrhea and menstrual problems. It can be used in bilongos where the removal of potency and lust is desired. It belongs to Mama Chola and Baluande.

Palo Torcido (Mouriri valenzuelana) is diabolically effective and fast when it comes to destroying someone's luck and bringing down their spiritual defenses by provoking distress in their life. It is sacred to Vence Bataya and Nkuyu.

Palo Vencedor/Satin Wood (Zanthoxylum arboreum) is an essential palo. It purifies in great amounts and attracts good fortune as it breaks down difficulties. It is sacred to Tiembla Tierra and Zarabanda.

Palo Vence Batalla/Bejuco (Guaco/Bignonia genus) is used to find success in all kinds of enterprises. It is victory itself finding ways where there are none. It belongs to Zarabanda and Vence Bataya.

Palo Verraco (Hypericum styphekiodes) is a palo that fights venereal diseases. It is said to be a palo that protects the genital area and always maintains the sensual fire. It is sacred to Mama Chola and Baluande.

Palo Vira Mundo, see *Palo Ramon*.

Palo Vencedor (Zanthoxylum pistacifolium) is balsamo or satin wood. It is great for purification, cleansings, to banish negativity and overcome difficulties. It can also be used as a tonic for weakness of the kidneys, heart and poor circulation. It is a wood with victorious qualities and belongs to Zarabanda and Vence Bataya.

Palo Yamao/Nkita American musk (Guarea trichiliodes) is most power-ful in works of attraction and binds and loses whatever one desires. It belongs to Centella, Mama Chola and Baluande.

Palo Yaya (Ozandra lanceolta) is a fundamental palo in prendas, espe-cially when making female ones and for Tiembla Tierra. It is the power of movement, war and magical virtues of many secret kinds.

GLOSSARY

Bilongo: A gathering of magical and powerful medicine that activates nkisi or a working. Also used in the sense of *making a work*.

Cascarilla: Powdered eggshell that serves as sacred chalk.

Chamba: The sacred water of fire of the palero.

Chicherekú: An image of wood or clay often placed at the centre or back of the nganga representing the ndoki of the nfumbi.

Fuá/fuidi/fuiri: Deceased, to die, dying.

Fula: Gunpowder.

Judio/Jewish: A reference to malefic and/or anti-Christian Palo practices.

Kalunga: Ocean, abyssal waters.

Kimbisa: A reference to *nature* in Kikongo. In Cuba the specific rama or order created by Andres Petit. It can also refer to the practical use of human bones or solely refer to the pact and consecration with nature.

Kindiambazo: A sorcerer, practitioner of Palo Mayombe.

Kinyumba: Bad, spirit, fiend, spectre.

Kiyumba: Cranium, skull.

Limpieza: A cleansing, a procedure to remove malefic influences from a person.

Lucero: The spirit of the forest that opens the veil for the dead to enter the world of the living.

Lukankazi: The spirit of fire, syncretised with the Devil.

Macuto: Talisman, charm, juju, can also be a prenda in miniature.

Mayombe: Considered to be the original form of Palo, defined by violent and sinister workings – in conformity with its dark reputation.

Mbele: Machete/blade.

Mbomba: Python, boa, Maju.

Menga: Blood.

Mpaka: This is a horn containing the very same elements as in the nganga and is a portable extension of the Nganga's soul. Ngangas can also be given in Mpakas. There is also the Mpaka vitit which is equipped with a mirror or glass used for divination.

Mpangui: Brother, friend, initiate.

Mpungo: Divine qualities that manifest in points of power in nature and the cosmos. They are often used in reference to specific qualities or *caminos*, roads of the nganga.

Mulemba: Lash, instrument of punishment.

Murumba: Palo Craft.

Musango: See *Bilongo*.

Mvumbi: Cadaver, ghost.

Ndoki: The malefic, vile and unpredictable aspect of existence, whether living or dead power, often with a negative connotation.

N*fumbi*/N*furi*: The deceased one that agrees to make part of the Nganga, often referred to as *the dog of the pot*. The nfumbe is represented by the physical bones and material history of someone who once was alive.

N*fumo*: Chief of ritual.

N*gangulero*: He or she who holds and works the Nganga.

N*ganga*: The spirit pot, the body of the nfumbe as it turns into nkisi.

N*gombe*: Meaning *oxen*, but is used in reference to mounting or possession.

N*gua*: Mother of ritual.

N*kanga*/N*kanda*: A magical binding.

N*kento*: Woman.

N*kisi*: The soul of the Nganga.

N*kita*: Spirits of the waters and the mountain.

N*kulo*: Ancestor.

N*kuto*: Hatred.

N*kutu*: Bag.

N*sunga*: Tobacco fumes.

N*sunsu*: Bird.

N*sunsu* N*dialongo*: Rooster.

N*sunsu* N*biola*: Hen.

N*sunsu* N*sambi*: Pigeon.

N*sunsu* N*suakara*: Guinea Hen, Guinea.

N*sunsu* K*iambico*: Duck.

N*sunsu* N*finda* C*olorao*: Pheasant.

Nsunsu Ndamba: Owl.

Nzambi: The Bantu name for God, referring to a creative impulse, often understood to be remote from human activities.

Nzo: Home, house, temple.

Tata Nganga: Palero who has received his nganga, for women the title is Yaya Nganga.

Tata Nkisi: A tata nganga with godchildren.

Vrillumba: A rama of Palo Mayombe.

CORRESPONDENCES BETWEEN

Baluande	Virgen de Regla
Brazo Fuerte	San Cristobal
Butá Nseke	San Silvestre and San Ramón Non Nato
Centella Ndoki	Virgen de la Candelaria
Chola Wengue	Virgen de la Caridad del Cobre
Iña Ñaába	Nuestra Señora de lãs Mercedes
Kabanga	San Francisco
Kisimbi Masa	Virgen de Regla
Lufo Kuyu	San Pedro y San Norberto
Lola	Nuestra Señora de lãs Mercedes
Majumbo Moúngu Mpungu	San Cosme y San Damián
Mama Kalunga	Virgen de Regla
Mama Canata	Virgen del Carmen
Mama Kengue	Virgen de las Mercedes
Mama Umba	Virgen de Regla
Mayumbo Moúngu	Virgen de Regla
Mpungu Mboma	Virgen de Regla
Mbumba Mamba	Virgen de Regla
Mpungo Lombua Mfula	San Francisco
Mpungo Lomboán Fula	San Francisco
Mpungu Mama Wanga	Virgen de la Candelaria
Mpungu Mama Wánga	Virgen de la Candelaria
Mukiama Muilo	Santa Bárbara
Mukiamamuilo	Santa Bárbara
Ndundu Yambaka	San Silvestre and San Ramón Non Nato
Nkita Kiamasa	Virgen de Regla

MPUNGO/NKISI & CHRISTIAN SAINTS

Nkita Kinseke	Spirits of mountain and savannah
Nkita Kitán	Santa Bárbara
Nkita Kuna Mamba	Virgen de Regla
Nkita Kuna Masa	Virgen de Regla
Nkita Kunamamba	Virgen de Regla
Nkita Kunamasa	Virgen de Regla
Nkuyo	El Ánima Sola del Purgatorio
{Nkuyo} Watariamba	San Norberto
Nsambi	God, the Creator
Nsasi	Santa Bárbara
Ntala y Nsamba	San Cosme y San Damián
Pandilanga	Jesus Christ
Pungo Dibudi	San Pedro
Pungo Kasimba	Virgen de Regla
Pungo Mama Wanga	Virgen de la Candelaria
Pungu Mfútila	San Lázaro
Pungún Fútila	San Lázaro
Sarabanda	San Miguel Arcángel
Sindaula	San Silvestre
Tata Fumbe	San Lázaro
Tiembla Tierra	Nuestra Señora de lās Mercedes
Watariamba	San Norberto
Yeyé	Nuestra Señora de lās Mercedes
Yolá/Lola	Nuestra Señora de lās Mercedes
Zarabanda	San Miguel Arcángel

SELECTED BIBLIOGRAPHY

ARÓSTEGUI, NATALIA, B & VILLEGAS, CARMEN G. D: *Ta Makuende Yaya y Las Reglas de Palo Monte*. Ediciones Union: Cuba, 1998.

BROWN, DAVID, H: *The Light Inside*. Smithsonian Books: US, 2003.

CABRERA, LYDIA: *La Regla Kimbisa del Santo Cristo del Buen Viaje*. Coleccion del Chicheriku em el Exílio: US, 1977.

CABRERA, LYDIA: *Reglas de Congo. Palo Monte Mayombe*. Coleccion del Chicheriku em el Exílio: US, 1979.

FIGAROLA, JOEL JAMES: *La Brujería Cubana: El Palo Monte*. Editorial Oriente: Cuba, 2009.

HEYWOOD, LINDA, M. (ED.): *Central Africans and Cultural Transformations in the American Diaspora*. Cambridge University Press: US, 2002.

JOHNSTON, SARAH, ILES: *Restless Dead*. University of California Press: US, 1999.

MACGAFFEY, WYATT: *Religion and Society in Central Africa: The Bakongo of Lower Zaire*. Univeristy of Chicago Press: US, 1986.

QUIROS-MORAN, DALIA: *Guide to Afro-Cuban Herbalism*. 1st Books. US, 2003.

THOMPSON, ROBERT, F: *Flash of the Spirit*. Vintage. US, 1983.

In addition a great number of unpublished tratados, librettas and manuals have been used.

THE MISA ESPIRITUAL

The spiritual mass makes part of what is called Palo Cruzado or mixed Palo, but nowadays it is a practice found useful by the majority of ramas and is frequently employed for a great variety of reasons. Its root lies in the work of Allan Kardec and his spiritist movement. The focus on communion with the departed has made this a viable practice to incorporate in the larger arcana of Palo Mayombe.

The misa is an elaboration of the *boveda* or 'spirits table'. To build a boveda and tend to it is not only something everybody can do, but it reaps benefits for everyone. The boveda gives us an opportunity to reconnect and dialogue with death. We can reestablish the communion with our ancestors and place ourselves under the guidance of the departed ones. What seems to often be the case in our modern times is that as a result of our broken ancestral chain, it is not necessarily ancestors, but rather spirit guides which come to the table. We are by this work establishing a spiritual ancestry and the more we allow spirit to move, without us superimposing our desires, the more helpful these guides can be in bringing us to our nzo – to our centre.

The boveda is simple to erect. You need a small table which you dress in a white cloth. At the centre you will place a bowl of water and a cross and around it nine smaller cups that you fill with water. A white candle and flowers should be present as well as coffee and a piece of bread. Tobacco fumes and perfumes make part of the calling and preparation of the session/temple. The misa is arranged in the same way.

When starting this practice it is wise to elect a given day and hour once a week where you attend to the boveda. You will then light the candle pour fresh water, give coffee and orient the items present on the table in accord with your ancestry. This means, give food and drinks and tokens you know your ancestors appreciated. Even if the effect is to draw spiritual guides, often unrelated to ones ancestry, it is important to call one's blood in the first instance and from this allow the work to unfold and the connection with spirits to be made.

It can take time before contact is made, but be diligent; a whisper can quickly grow into visions and powerful dreams of truth. Allow the gifts on the boveda to rest until the next day when you discard them, preferably directly on the earth. Be attentive to inspirations and instincts quickening. This is a work that stimulates a greater awareness.

The Misa Espiritual is different in that it requires possession of the medium by the spiritual guides. A typical misa will have the medium smoking a cigar and anointing him or herself with perfume whilst calling his or her spirit guides. The possession can be soft or violent, but quite frequently the trained medium is moved by spirit.

You can do this with prayers from the heart, songs, learnt prayers or what can be seen as conjurations. There are many paths towards the receptive state. A selection of songs/prayers traditionally used are presented here, the first mambo is for paleros, and spiritual practitioners start with the second mambo:

BUENAS NOCHES

> *Pero Buenas Noches si son de Noche Mayombe*
> *E com Licencia Nfinda Kalunga Mayombe*
> *E com Licencia Nfinda Anabutos Mayombe*
> *E com Licencia lo Zarabanda Mayombe*
> *E com Licencia lo Madre Nganga Mayombe*
> *E com Licencia de mi Padrino Mayombe*
> *E com Licencia de (name of nfumbe) Mayombe*
> *E com Licencia de (name of nganga) Mayombe*
> *Primerio Nzambi, Que to los cosas Mayombe*
> *Pero Buenas Noches Palo, si son de Noche Mayombe*
> *E yo saludando lo Mayomberos, Mayombe*
> *E yo saludando los nijos de nkisi de Mayombe*
> *E yo creo em dios Yo creo em diablo Mayombe*
> *Que lo Buenos dias, sin son de dia Mayombe*
> *Que lo Bueno tarde, si son de tarde Mayombe*
> *Que lo buen monazo, pa to lo mundo Mayombe*
> *Pero Buenas Noches pa to lo Nfumbe Mayombe*

CONGO MÍO

Congo mío, ven de los montes
yo te llamo a laborar,
cuando vengas, ven despacio
paso a paso a trabajar.
Yo te llamo y tu respondes
yo te llamo de verdad,
yo te llamo congo en bembé
yo te llamo pa' jugar.
Yo te veo en la maleza
trabajando material,
con tu cazuela de barro
y tu empaca pa' mirar.
Tú te llamas como quieras
tu nombre no quieres dar
lo que quiero, congo mío,
no nos dejes de ayudar;
lo que quiero, congo mío,
no nos dejes de ayudar.
Congo, ven congo a trabajar.
Congo mío sal del monte, vamos a jugar.
Congo, ven congo a trabajar,
que como quiera yo te llamo para laborar.
Congo, ven congo a trabajar,
que estoy buscando un congo bueno para laborar.
Congo, ven congo a trabajar,
ay, paso franco yo te llamo aquí a laborar.
Congo, ven congo a trabajar,
que congo mío sal del monte, vamos a jugar.
Congo, ven congo a trabajar,
a güiri güiri güiri a güiri güiri co
a güiri güiri güiri a güiri güiri co
yo ando buscando un congo que pueda más que yo
a güiri güiri güiri a güiri güiri co

a güiri güiri güiri a güiri güiri co
yo ando buscando un congo que pueda más que yo
que yo ando buscando uno, yo ando buscando dos
yo ando buscando uno, yo ando buscando dos
ando buscando un congo que pueda más que yo
a güiri güiri güiri a güiri güiri co
a güiri güiri güiri a güiri güiri co
yo ando buscando un congo que pueda más que yo
ay, yo ando buscando un congo
que pueda más que yo
que yo busco hasta a José
que pueda más que yo
que yo busco a mi gabán
que pueda más que yo
ay a San Lucero, llamo
que pueda más que yo
ay, yo ando buscando un congo
que pueda más que yo
ay, yo ando buscando un congo
que pueda más que yo
a güiri güiri güiri a güiri güiri co
a güiri güiri güiri a güiri güiri co
yo ando buscando un congo que pueda más que yo
a güiri güiri güiri a güiri güiri co
a güiri güiri güiri a güiri güiri co
yo ando buscando un congo que pueda más que yo

EL SANTÍSIMO

Sea el Santísimo, sea.
Sea el Santísimo, sea.
Madre mía de la Caridad,
ayúdanos, ampáranos
en el nombre de Dios, ay Dios

Sea el Santísimo, sea.
Sea el Santísimo, sea.
Madre mía de la Caridad,
ayúdanos, ampáranos
en el nombre de Dios, ay Dios

AVE MARÍA

Oh, del cielo ha bajado la madre de Dios,
cantemos un Ave a su protección.
Ave, Ave, Ave María.
Ave, Ave, Ave María.
Oh, María, madre mía,
oh, consuelo celestial
amparadnos y guiadnos
a la patria celestial.
Ave, Ave, Ave María.
Ave, Ave, Ave María.
Viva María, viva José,
viva esta obra espiritual
pues María concebida
¿cuál pecado original?
Ave, Ave, Ave María.
Ave, Ave, Ave María.
Si en el cielo tres estrellas
iluminan la verdad
es la fe, es la esperanza
y la hermana caridad.
Ave, Ave, Ave María.
Ave, Ave, Ave María.
Ay Ave, Ave, Ave María.
Ave, Ave, Ave María.
Ave, Ave, Ave María.
Ave, Ave, Ave María.

Santa María en la Luna,
Santa Isabel en el Sol.
Y alrededor de nosotros
no quiero perturbación.
Santa María en la Luna,
Santa Isabel en el Sol.
Y alrededor de nosotros
no quiero perturbación.
Yo llamo un ser y no viene,
lo llamo en nombre de Dios.
Yo llamo a las siete potencias,
no quiero perturbación.
Santa María en la Luna
Santa Isabel en el Sol
Y alrededor de nosotros
no quiero perturbación
San María Madre,
Santa Teresa de Jesús
por ahí viene un Misionero
y viene buscando luz.
Santa María Madre
Santa Teresa de Jesús,
por ahí viene un Misionero
y viene buscando luz.
Ay, trabajar, ay trabajar,
oye, laborar media unidad;
laborando se recibe
fe, esperanza y caridad.
Trabajar, trabajar,
trabajar media unidad
laborando se recibe
fe, esperanza y caridad
Pero trabajar, ay trabajar,
oye, trabaja así media unidad;
que con los muertos recibimos

fe, esperanza y caridad.
Trabajar, trabajar,
trabajar media unidad;
(espiritistas a laborar)
laborando se recibe
fe, esperanza y caridad.
Que laborando se recibe
fe, esperanza y caridad.
Con los muertos recibimos
fe, esperanza y caridad.
Oye, trabajar, ay trabajar,
oye, trabaja así media unidad;
laborando se recibe
fe, esperanza y caridad, tú ves.
Trabajar, trabajar,
trabajar media unidad
laborando se recibe
fe, esperanza y caridad.

CONGO DE GUINEA

Congo de Guinea soy, ay si las buenas noches criollo,
congo de Guinea soy, ay las buenas noches criollo.
Yo deja mi hueso allá, yo viene a hacer caridad,
yo deja mi hueso allá, yo viene a hacer caridad.
Congo de Guinea soy, buenas noches criollo,
congo de Guinea soy, buenas noches criollo.
Yo deja mi hueso allá, yo viene a hacer caridad,
yo deja mi hueso allá, yo viene a hacer caridad.
Ay, congo de Guinea soy, ay si las buenas noches criollo,
Ay, congo de Guinea soy, ay las buenas noches criollo.
Yo deja mi hueso allá, yo viene a hacer caridad,
yo deja mi hueso allá, yo viene a hacer caridad.
Congo de Guinea soy, buenas noches criollo,

congo de Guinea soy, buenas noches criollo.
Yo deja mi hueso allá, yo viene a hacer caridad,
yo deja mi hueso allá, yo viene a hacer caridad.
El mundo de los misterios, yo voy en busca de un ser,
ay, del mundo de los misterios, yo voy en busca de un ser.
Piango piango bajo a la tierra,
piango piango a cumplir misión.
Piango piango bajo a la tierra,
piango piango a cumplir misión.
El mundo de los misterios, yo voy en busca de un ser,
Del mundo de los misterios, yo voy en busca de un ser.
Piango piango bajo a la tierra,
piango piango a cumplir misión.
Piango piango bajo a la tierra,
piango piango a cumplir misión.
Pero del mundo de los misterios, ay yo voy en busca de un ser,
Ay del mundo de los misterios, yo voy en busca de un ser.
Piango piango yo bajo a la tierra,
piango piango a cumplir misión.
Piango piango yo bajo a la tierra,
piango piango a cumplir misión.
El mundo de los misterios, yo voy en busca de un ser,
Del mundo de los misterios, yo voy en busca de un ser.
Piango piango bajo a la tierra,
piango piango a cumplir misión.
Piango piango bajo a la tierra,
piango piango a cumplir misión.
Ay, yo vengo de Ina Ina, pero yo vengo de Olodumare.
Yo vengo de Ina Ina, pero yo vengo de Olodumare.
Cuando un congo es de belleza, yo saludo sus collares.
Cuando un congo es de belleza, yo saludo sus collares.
Yo vengo de Ina Ina, yo vengo de Olodumare.
Yo vengo de Ina Ina, yo vengo de Olodumare.
Cuando un congo es de belleza, yo saludo sus collares.
Cuando un congo es de belleza, yo saludo sus collares.

Pero , yo vengo de Ina Ina, ay yo vengo de Olodumare.
Ay, yo vengo de Ina Ina, pero yo vengo de Olodumare.
Cuando un congo es de belleza, yo saludo sus collares.
Cuando un congo es de belleza, yo saludo sus collares. Mi Dios.
Yo vengo de Ina Ina, yo vengo de Olodumare.
Yo vengo de Ina Ina, yo vengo de Olodumare.
Cuando un congo es de belleza, yo saludo sus collares.
Cuando un congo es de belleza, yo saludo sus collares.
Vamos a comer, vamos a hacer un dulce;
tapa la cazuela que sabroso esta el dulce.
Eh, vamos a comer, mi congo, vamos a hacer un dulce;
tapa la cazuela que sabroso esta el dulce.
Eh, congo va a comer, muerta va a hacer un dulce;
tapa la cazuela que sabroso esta el dulce.
Vamos a comer, vamos a hacer un dulce;
tapa la cazuela que sabroso esta el dulce.

ADIOS

Mambe
Dios
Mambe
Dios
Mambe Dios
Mambe
Adios
Amen

During the misa it is the medium who is in charge and is using mambos and prayers according to their functional and rama. The songs given here constitute a sort of core practice that has proved efficient in developing the receptive ability necessary to receive the spirits.

There is no hard and fast rule to this, but the discipline of the boveda if done with diligence will over time develop the mediumistic abilities needed to be a truthful vinculum for the spirit guides.

APOLOGIA

Nsala Malecum!

In the name of Nzambi and all mpungo wise and manifest in nkisi all over creation I bring this apology.

The objective of this book has been to give to the world an account of a cult/religion that is often viewed with bias or as simply sinister. It is at the same time a coded handbook for the practitioner and a faithful presentation of how my experience of Palo Mayombe has matured over the years.

I am aware that some paleros will think I have revealed too much and others not enough. To this I will say that what has been revealed is necessary, and that the secrets are well veiled within codes and signs. My oath is to the best of my ability still kept in the desire of sharing in order to counter the mass of disinformation. I will say to those paleros and yayas who think I have revealed too much that the secret is truly outside the power of language to communicate. Secrets hinted at here are only revealed when they are understood in light of the knowledge given as a consequence of one's initiation.

To those who think I should have said more; I have tried here to give a faithful testament and presentation of Palo Mayombe being as truthful as possible to the diversity of ramas and viewpoints. It is a memoriam to my Tatas and also a token of thanksgiving to those faithful and unfaithful brothers and sisters who have aided me somehow along the road of understanding. The path towards understanding Palo Maybome has been crooked indeed, and on the path of discovery guides and deceivers have been equally important. You who have been guiding me properly know who you are and to all of you I owe gratitude.

I believe the core of Palo Mayombe is rooted in the pact we make with the nfumbe. This opens up a plethora of insights. Nfumbe makes part of a great array of disincarnate intelligences and spirits that makes our life understandable – and for bringing this knowledge to the world I make no excuse. As such I have brought this book out in the hope that it will serve the greater community of paleros well, and give a more precise and considered idea of the complexity of our wonderful religion/cult for the non-Spanish speaking readers and seekers.

Malecum Nsala!

Tata Remolino Quatro Nsila Changani Culumba Batalla Vence Guerra
Viramundo

INDEX

A

Abakuá societies 5, 34, 35, 36, 51, 52

Ancestral memory 2, 41, 65, 110, 122, 156

Angoro 41, 42, 140

Angoromea 41, 42, 140

B

Ba'Kongo 3, 4, 5, 6, 8

Baluande viii, 42, 44, 110, 111, 134, 136, 150, 151, 171, 176, 177, 180, 181, 182, 183, 188, 189, 190, 192, 193, 194, 195, 199, 200, 202, 203, 208

Bilongo 13, 14, 15, 25, 72, 83, 106, 123, 133, 142, 145, 147, 149, 153, 154, 186, 187, 194, 196, 205

C

Cabrera, Lydia 50, 87, 158

Candomblé 5

Cão, Diogo 4, 6

Cauldron i, 70, 156

Ceiba 73, 79, 95, 96, 98, 101, 108, 121, 123, 142, 155, 162, 175, 176

Centella viii, 44, 74, 83, 104, 106, 107, 108, 113, 119, 121, 122, 138, 139, 149, 150, 153, 156, 165, 172, 174, 175, 176, 180, 182, 183, 185, 186, 189, 192, 193, 196, 197, 198, 199, 201, 202, 203, 208

Christian influence ii

Christianity vii, 3, 6, 7, 8, 10, 13, 15, 16, 18, 21, 22, 32, 51

Cobayende viii, 73, 74, 113, 114, 115, 126, 136, 143, 152, 153, 154, 156, 165, 172, 174, 175, 177, 179, 180, 182, 183, 184, 185, 187, 188, 189, 190, 192, 193, 195, 196, 198

G

Gurunfinda viii, 42, 44, 73, 93, 117, 118, 119, 126, 129, 134, 136, 172, 173, 176, 181, 183, 190, 191, 193, 194, 195, 197, 198, 200, 201

I

Iboga initiation 11

Imbangala 26, 27, 28, 29

J

João II, King 4, 6

K

Kalunga 2, 3, 4, 10, 11, 22, 23, 25, 42, 44, 48, 51

Kilundu 12

Kimbanda 5, 6, 41